Easy Living
One-Story Designs™

Over 250 Designs
For Single-Level Living

From 962 to 3,734 Square Feet

design basics inc®
HOME PLAN DESIGN SERVICE

Dennis Brozak   Linda Reimer
CO-PUBLISHERS

EDITOR Kevin Blair

PLANS EDITOR Tina Libe

WRITER Joyce Brown

GRAPHIC DESIGNERS Jeff Dedlow
Heather Guthrie
Beverly Nelligan
Annette Guy

RENDERING ILLUSTRATORS Shawn Doherty
Perry M. Gauthier
Gerald Metzger
George MacDonald (dec.)

TECHNICAL ADVISERS Carl Cuozzo
Rob Phillips
Tom Clark

CIRCULATION MANAGER Priscilla Ivey

Easy Living
One-Story Designs™

IS PUBLISHED BY:
DESIGN BASICS PUBLICATIONS
11112 JOHN GALT BLVD., OMAHA, NE 68137
www.designbasics.com
info@designbasics.com

CHIEF EXECUTIVE OFFICER Dennis Brozak

PRESIDENT Linda Reimer

DIRECTOR OF MARKETING Kevin Blair

BUSINESS DEVELOPMENT Paul Foresman

CONTROLLER Janie Murnane

EDITOR-IN-CHIEF Bruce Arant

The Mayberry, Plan #2761-9G, as seen
on the cover was built by Mark Hughes
Construction. More information on the
plan is available on page 18.

HOME PLAN DESIGN SERVICE

Library of Congress Control Number:
00-133407
ISBN: 1-892150-21-2

Easy Living
One-Story Designs™

Plan #	Plan Name	Sq. Ft.	Page
2568	Avery	962	8
1184	Lorain	975	8
1129	Calumet	1125	9
6740	Balentine	1142	9
8161	Morton Grove	1162	10
8163	Trinity Acres	1162	10
5479	Oakfield	1191	11
2376	Dover	1205	11
8093	Kirby Farm	1212	12
2825	Laurell	1261	12
24045	Glenco	1263	13
1551	Logan	1271	13
8128	Redwood Lane	1279	14
8092	Summit Point	1295	14
969	Benton	1305	15
3907	Reynolds	1316	15
8164	Sabino Canyon	1333	16
6731	Tollefson	1334	16
6727	Hudson	1337	17
5180	Holbrook	1339	17
3102	Aspen	1339	18
2761	Mayberry	1341	18
1963	Kaplin	1347	19
24048	Cartwright	1359	19
8091	Winter Woods	1360	20
5464	Janssen	1379	20
5467	Pineview	1385	21
2263	Dalton	1385	21
8013	Gabriel Bay	1392	22
1267	Westbury	1392	22
24035	Lindale	1395	23
8165	Sarasota Falls	1398	23
6729	Sedgewick	1406	24
8129	Cedar Falls	1420	24
3010	Quimby	1422	25
6728	Oberlin	1422	25
1379	Pendleton	1429	26
8089	Chandler Hills	1433	26
5476	Culverton	1437	27
6726	Pellman	1446	27
8160	Bradford Pointe	1449	28
2173	Fraser	1451	28
8090	Spring Valley	1453	29
5034	Payson	1472	29
3260	Kirby	1478	30
3019	Kelsey	1479	30
2550	Vinton	1486	31
6725	Harman	1495	31
6734	Kenton	1495	32
2300	Adair	1496	32
6703	Conway	1498	33
2553	Gifford	1499	33
6724	Behrens	1506	34
6271	Torrington	1509	34
679	Quincy	1511	35
8015	Copper Creek	1515	35
6265	Edinborough	1517	36
3555	Laramy	1518	36
8088	Shadow Pines	1520	37
6807	San Pablo	1528	37
24029	Feldon	1539	38
24051	Cabrie	1541	38
5035	Canton	1552	39
3127	Haley	1554	39
1770	Bayley	1556	40
5460	Sullivan	1558	40
2196	Granite	1561	41
8159	Skyline Woods	1562	41
6735	Coventry	1570	42
5457	Ashcroft	1577	42
3899	Bradshaw	1577	43
8087	Collins Falls	1579	43
2537	Tahoe	1580	44
2324	Oakridge	1583	44
8158	Jacobs Bay	1593	45
3578	Stonybrook	1595	45
1017	Kirwin	1598	46
2291	Bradley	1599	46
1767	Rosebury	1604	47
2923	Sutton	1622	47
8080	Maple Grove	1628	48
8079	Belle Harbor	1633	48
5466	Somerdale	1636	49
2377	Leighton	1636	49
3915	Ithaca	1643	50
5179	Spenlow	1650	50
2818	Orchard	1651	51
5001	Anson	1653	51
2907	Ashley	1658	52
5080	Thomaston	1660	52
6804	Tucson	1666	53
2290	Monterey	1666	53
5177	Cedric	1679	54
3889	Montclare	1684	54
5471	Whittaker	1686	55
8016	Jennys Brook	1691	55
24017	Margo	1694	56
1262	Covington	1696	56
1032	Monte Vista	1697	57
3919	Dunbar	1699	57
8168	Sonora Springs	1705	58
8078	North Cliffs	1707	58
2355	Waverly	1710	59
5473	Woodridge	1712	59
8069	Quail Hollow	1729	60
2212	Seville	1735	60
9187	Creekbend Manor	1751	61
8068	Hancock Ridge	1751	61
4948	Bradbury	1758	62
24003	Tuxford	1762	62
24026	Warren	1767	63
5454	Anandale	1768	63
5459	Langston	1772	64
8067	River Oaks	1775	64
3577	Bennett	1782	65
6732	Westfall	1784	65
5465	Christine	1790	66
6723	Bostwick	1791	66

Plan #	Plan Name	Sq. Ft.	Page	Plan #	Plan Name	Sq. Ft.	Page
3298	Ogden	1793	67	8045	Coopers Farm	2151	100
3587	Charleston	1796	67	5036	Cameron	2167	101
8066	Hidden Acres	1805	68	2326	Greensboro	2172	101
5181	Vautrin	1806	68	3005	Wrenwood	2186	102
3006	Grayson	1806	69	3598	Brentwood	2187	102
1559	Bancroft	1808	69	5498	Hartwell	2188	103
24040	Highland	1810	70	3128	Alvarado	2199	103
8018	Forest Glen	1815	70	9206	Winston Court	2203	104
24020	Brooks	1819	71	6268	Knollwood	2205	104
3887	Winfield	1821	71	9185	Longworth Estate	2211	105
8059	Indian Springs	1842	72	4998	Holden	2227	105
7214	Belwood	1843	72	2934	Osage	2233	106
24012	Larose	1849	73	8121	Nelsons Landing	2241	106
2461	Shawnee	1850	73	5141	Enfield	2242	107
8058	Morgan Creek	1852	74	8017	Jackson Acres	2246	107
4953	Morenci	1853	74	24002	Hanson	2250	108
3894	Webber	1864	75	1388	Beaumont	2254	108
3299	Tatum	1873	75	9189	Alexander Court	2256	109
9198	Windrush Estate	1876	76	5516	Wildwood	2266	109
3891	Stockville	1883	76	3523	Blanchard	2274	110
3879	Thomasville	1885	77	2321	Aberdeen	2276	110
5507	Elrose	1886	77	8120	Emerald Harbor	2293	111
2799	Hawthorne	1887	78	24030	Royston	2297	111
5135	Hayden	1894	78	8048	Sydney Lane	2298	112
6809	Laredo	1895	79	7215	Wheatland	2299	112
1748	Sinclair	1911	79	3058	Montgomery	2311	113
8019	Hunters Crossing	1919	80	2651	Fairway	2317	113
5090	Simeon	1920	80	9207	Briar Manor	2331	114
5496	McClellan	1924	81	24033	Malone	2334	114
9201	Waterside Estate	1926	81	2459	Harcourt	2335	115
5506	Springvale	1931	82	2192	Melbourne	2355	115
5515	Caldwell	1941	82	3524	Tangent	2366	116
2384	Surrey	1948	83	7213	Jinson	2383	116
3553	Glenmorrie	1960	83	9191	Crescent Court	2393	117
8046	Laurel Grove	1967	84	3514	Nottsbury	2399	117
6803	Santa Fe	1970	84	8044	Falcon Point	2404	118
4644	Elving	1971	85	9159	Edgewater Court	2409	118
3276	Cedardale	1973	85	6801	Tempe	2411	119
3031	Jonesville	1978	86	1232	Evanston	2422	119
24021	Barber	1980	86	24014	Pearl	2451	120
1539	Mansfield	1996	87	2778	Comstock	2456	120
8047	Millers Way	1999	87	8023	Eagles Ridge	2467	121
2361	Summerwood	2015	88	2472	Hillsboro	2470	121
3892	Tecumseh	2035	88	2206	Hawkesbury	2498	122
4951	Aldrich	2039	89	3535	Hallmark	2504	122
5490	Dennison	2040	89	2652	Lawrence	2512	123
9171	Westcott Manor	2040	90	9199	Kingwood Showcase	2517	123
8122	Alberta Falls	2042	90	3057	Ascott	2538	124
2843	Atwood	2047	91	2581	Eastridge	2558	124
3139	Foxboro	2053	91	5505	Claire	2579	125
4208	Creighton	2057	92	5503	Briarton	2586	125
2222	Plainview	2068	92	3045	Royale	2598	126
24001	Richdale	2073	93	6806	San Carlos	2647	126
8118	Crooked Creek	2079	93	5513	Lauren	2650	127
3303	Richardson	2083	94	2834	Del Ray	2651	127
2454	Pickford	2093	94	3483	Westmont	2655	128
8022	Prarie View	2117	95	9200	Stonelake Manor	2679	129
3196	Galloway	2120	95	6802	Vista	2716	130
24038	Clarkson	2126	96	2844	Coronado	2716	131
3597	Concorde	2132	96	5003	Saybrooke	2750	132
1689	Newman	2133	97	2580	Raleigh	2775	133
3145	Gregory	2141	97	3033	Avalon	2899	134
5508	Karoline	2143	98	3440	Cornell	2988	135
24027	Oakland	2144	98	3018	Shiloh	2994	136
8119	Harvest Run	2144	99	9120	The Whitmore	3312	137
2848	Roxbury	2148	99	9118	Villa De Baca	3590	138
2213	Essex	2149	100	9139	Autumn View	3734	139

Since 1983, Design Basics has been bringing people home with many of America's most popular home plans. Our company began as a custom home plan design firm for the professional builders of our local community, Omaha, NE. As the popularity of our designs increased, we expanded our focus from designing for the local market only, to designing plans that would be adaptable anywhere. Since then builder, as well as consumer, interest in our plans has grown tremendously in all 50 states and countries around the world. Today we are one of the nation's largest home plan design services, offering a variety of home plans, as well as products and services which include: color renderings, estimator's material lists, plan changes and more.

Whether it's one of our home plans, a product or service, we take pride in serving you with our very best. It's all a part of our culminating efforts to lead people to their dreams of home.

"Bringing People Home"

More information on plan #2652, the Lawrence is available on page 123.

Built By: Tweedt Engineering & Construction

ONE-STORY HOMES
past and present

More information on plan #1689, the Newman is available on page 97.

Today's one-story homes have their roots in the 1930s when some creative architects in California designed the first one-stories known as "ranches." World War II put a halt to most residential building before the style caught on. But by the end of the war, the time was ripe for the "rambling ranch" to become the ultimate symbol of the American dream.

Before the war, most people were dependent on streetcars and buses for transportation. Neighborhoods consisted of compact houses on small lots so people wouldn't have to walk too far to their stops. As soldiers returned home to start families, a tremendous housing boom took off. With more and more families owning automobiles, it became practical for neighborhoods to

spread out. The stage was set for ranch homes to re-shape the American landscape.

These one-story homes reflected changes taking place in society in general, from formal to casual. America's growing love of the outdoors made their picture windows and sliding patio doors added attractions. Even more so, busy lifestyles enjoyed the convenience of one-story living and the practicality of fewer stairs.

While one-story homes have remained a popular mainstay in American architecture, they've recently enjoyed a tremendous resurgence. Baby boomers looking forward to retirement years are choosing one-story homes for their ease of accessibility. But many younger families are also seeking them out. Perhaps it's because they desire more

Built By: Fairview Homes. More information on plan #2461, the Shawnee is available on page 73.

Built By: Jacobs Const. More information on plan #8013, the Gabriel Bay is available on page 22.

TODAY'S ONE-STORY HOMES ARE
better than ever –
WITH INTERESTING ROOF LINES, HIGHER CEILINGS, OPEN FLOOR PLANS, BIGGER CLOSETS
and more style.

Built By: Decker Building Co. More information on plan #3019, the Kelsey is available on page 30.

permanence in their lives. They want a home that will grow and adapt, so they won't have to move to a different house every time their needs change.

Today's one-story homes are designed better than ever -- with interesting roof lines, higher ceilings, open floor plans, bigger closets and more style. Improved technology has made it possible to create finished lower levels that are beautiful living spaces and bare little resemblance to basements of the past. Many builders now incorporate higher basement walls, daylight windows and walk-out designs to produce bright, light-filled lower levels. In addition, new building materials are allowing greater open spans with fewer support beams.

To say the least, the "ranch" has improved with age and Easy Living One-Story Designs proudly presents 252 of the very best. ■

More information on plan #3006, the Grayson is available on page 68.

Built By: RLR Construction

new additions to an
Old Favorite

The original Easy Living One-Story Designs consisted of designs from our stylish Gold Seal™ Collection, our value-oriented Heartland Home Plans Collection™, and luxurious plans from Carmichael & Dame. One-hundred new plans have been added to this edition including designs from W. L. Martin and Carmichael & Dame.

These homes reflect the latest building trends and expanded needs of today's home buyers. They feature more "flex" rooms which can be converted to function in different ways as buyers' needs change. Additionally, an emphasis has been placed on larger gathering areas and the availability of bonus rooms and finished rooms over garages.

Included in this edition are plans rich in architectural tradition from our Nostalgia Home Plans Collection™. Special detailing, common in stately homes of the past, gives these designs a sense of craftsmanship and character. Quaint alcoves, built-in display cabinets, master suite sitting rooms, dropped soffits, cornices and columns contribute a sense of quality found in vintage homes.

Seven plans from our Terra Cotta Collection™ offer distinctive southwestern styling -- dressed in stucco walls, clay tile roofs and trimmed with timbers and wrought iron. To heighten the regional feel of these homes, we've developed more outdoor living spaces with large porches, patios, courtyards and verandas.

The Hometown Collection™ represents our newest plans. Although these designs feature simple foundation lines, they also enjoy interesting elevations with roomy front porches, quaint trim and nicely pitched roofs. Interiors are informal. Minimum ceilings of nine feet and open floor plans create a sense of spaciousness.

Within the Hometown Collection™, we've incorporated three universally designed plans which meet commercial codes for accessibility. These stylish homes include larger halls, doorways, closets and bathrooms. Rooms are spacious enough to allow ample wheelchair clearance even after furniture is placed. Kitchens are equipped with more counter space, cabinets include pull-out work trays, center islands feature clearance space beneath them and built-in ovens are located at the proper height for use from a wheelchair. In addition, garages are larger with doors high enough to accommodate accessible vans. These universally designed plans can be found on pages 34, 62 and 70.

Our original version of Easy Living One-Story Designs enjoyed long-standing popularity. But with all the extras we've added to this new and improved edition, we believe you'll enjoy it even more. ■

Total Square Footage: 1337

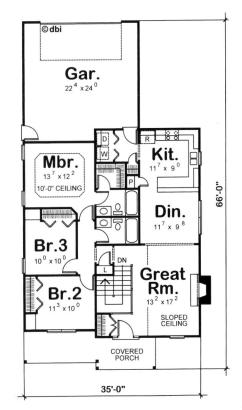

NOTE: 9 FT. MAIN LEVEL WALLS

- open great room includes coat closet and cozy fireplace

- wrap-around kitchen enjoys two pantries, window over sink and roomy snack bar

- doors hide the washer and dryer to provide a tidy entrance from the garage complete with coat closet

- master bedroom features corner windows, special ceiling detail and large walk-in closet

- built-in desks enhance both secondary bedrooms

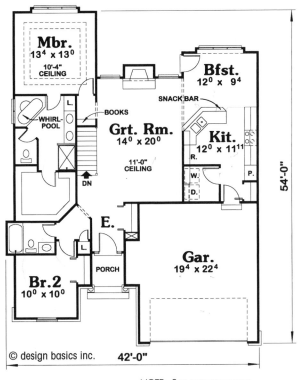

NOTE: 9 FT. MAIN LEVEL WALLS

Total Square Footage: 1339

- an angled counter in the kitchen helps define the space and organize the working areas

- the large great room draws guests inside with its fireplace and access to a nearby bookshelf

- a full bath serves the main floor as well as the second bedroom

- the garage offers an alcove to build a work bench or shelves

3102-9G ASPEN

PRICE CODE 13

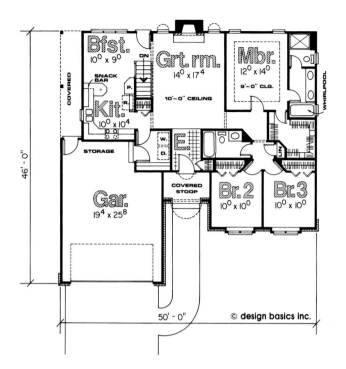

Total Square Footage: 1339

- arched entry highlights brick and siding elevation

- great room with arched windows creates beautiful view from entry

- window at sink overlooks versatile covered area outside

- kitchen features large snack bar and convenient access to spacious utility room

- master suite contains generous walk-in and whirlpool bath with compartmented stool and shower

2761-9G MAYBERRY

PRICE CODE 13

Total Square Footage: 1341

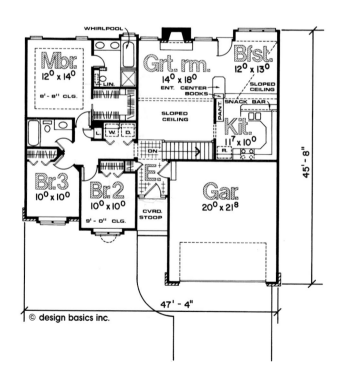

- sloped ceiling, and fireplace flanked by windows expand the great room

- kitchen is exceptionally well planned, featuring large pantry, two lazy Susans and snack bar serving the dinette

- strategically located TV cabinet/entertainment center affords viewing from great room, dinette or kitchen

- master suite features large walk-in closet and deluxe bath area

800-947-7526

design basics inc.
HOME PLAN DESIGN SERVICE

Total Square Footage: 1347

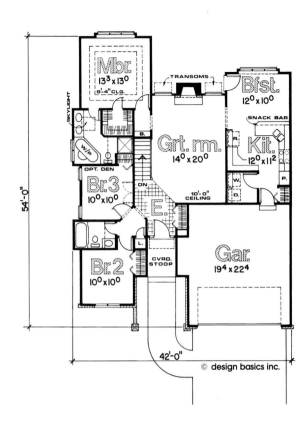

© design basics inc.

- a 10-foot-high ceiling visually expands the entry and great room

- open staircase for versatile future finished basement

- bedroom #3 easily becomes a den with French doors off entry

- picture windows with transoms above flank handsome fireplace in great room

- skylit master dressing/bath area features double vanity and whirlpool on angle under window

24048-9G CARTWRIGHT
PRICE CODE 13

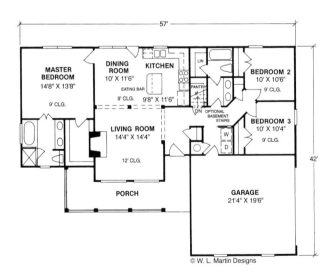

© W. L. Martin Designs

Total Square Footage: 1359

- a wrap-around porch leads inside where the living room is visible from the entry

- the large size of the master bedroom makes it a great get-away spot where one can enjoy its abundant amenities

- two additional bedrooms share a compartmented bath with walk-in linen closet

- the laundry room is near the secondary bedrooms and across from a full bath

8091-9G Winter Woods

PRICE CODE 13

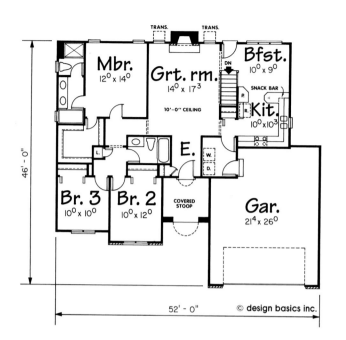

Total Square Footage: 1360

- a wide covered stoop is substantial enough for a chair

- wrapping counters in the kitchen help quickly access all that is needed to cook

- amenities in the master suite include a large walk-in closet, sunlit tub and dual-sink vanity

5464-9G Janssen

PRICE CODE 13

Total Square Footage: 1379

NOTE: 9 FT. MAIN LEVEL WALLS

- a private covered porch offers an escape off the master bedroom

- the study is flexible as a formal dining room

- symmetrical arches frame an open great room

- an island counter forms a working triangle from the stove to the sink in the kitchen

- a front porch with stone accents reveals the relaxed candor of this one-story home

CUSTOMIZE
any home plan

Total Square Footage: 1385

- a walk-in pantry and island counter make the kitchen a convenient place to work

- the spacious dining area offers more than accomodation for family, friends and guests

- an isolated location was designed for the den, which will easily accomodate a home computer and work center

- an attractive portico gives a touch of sophistication to this two-car garage

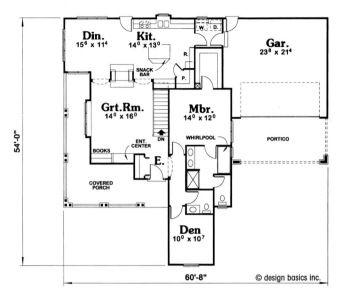

NOTE: 9 FT. MAIN LEVEL WALLS

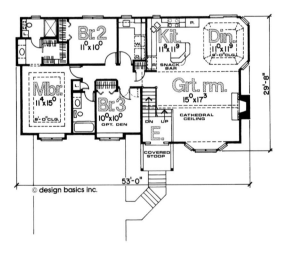

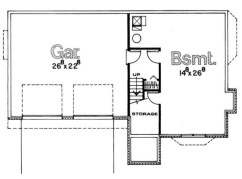

Total Square Footage: 1385

- vaulted ceiling and windows on corner angles enhance the dinette

- amenities in kitchen include a snack bar on an island counter plus corner sink and pantry

- convenient main floor laundry room offers window and soaking sink

- versatile bedroom #3 can become den by adding French doors

- a compartmented stool and shower and walk-in closet serve the master dressing area

8013-9G GABRIEL BAY

PRICE CODE 13

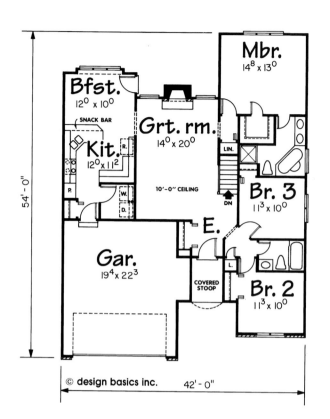

© design basics inc.   42'-0"

Total Square Footage: 1392

- sceondary bedrooms could be converted to office space or hobby room
- the master retreat offers a corner tub for basking in relaxation
- open kitchen and breakfast area are great for casual entertaining

1267-9G WESTBURY

PRICE CODE 13

Total Square Footage: 1392

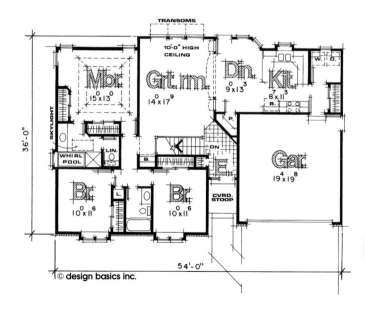

© design basics inc.

- master bedroom with vaulted ceiling includes his-and-her closets, whirlpool tub, skylight and plant ledges plus compartmented stool
- great room enjoys volume ceiling and floor-to-ceiling windows
- beautiful arches adorn the great room and dinette
- garage/utility entrance with closet makes carrying groceries in from the car much easier

CUSTOMIZE
any home plan

design basics inc.
HOME PLAN DESIGN SERVICE

Total Square Footage: 1395

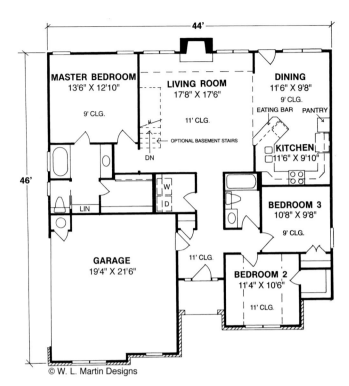

MASTER BEDROOM
13'6" X 12'10"

9' CLG.

LIVING ROOM
17'8" X 17'6"

11' CLG.

OPTIONAL BASEMENT STAIRS

DN

DINING
11'6" X 9'8"

9' CLG.

EATING BAR   PANTRY

KITCHEN
11'6" X 9'10"

LIN

W
D

BEDROOM 3
10'8" X 9'8"

9' CLG.

44'

46'

GARAGE
19'4" X 21'6"

11' CLG.

BEDROOM 2
11'4" X 10'6"

11' CLG.

© W. L. Martin Designs

- the use of brick on the front exterior of this home offers low maintenance

- u-shaped counters in the kitchen create an efficient work area and offer service to the living room

- the dining room features a double window and backyard access

- the large master bedroom has an adjoining bath with walk-in closet and tub beneath a window

- bedroom 2 offers the visual appeal of an arched window and sloped ceiling

8165-9G SARASOTA FALLS
PRICE CODE 13

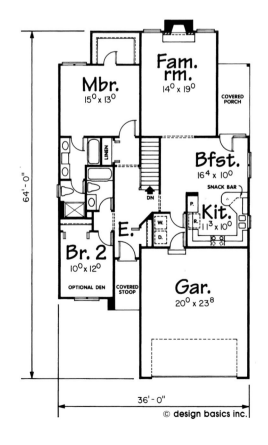

Mbr.
15⁰ x 13⁰

Fam. rm.
14⁰ x 19⁰

COVERED PORCH

LINEN

Bfst.
16⁴ x 10⁰

SNACK BAR

DN

Kit.
11³ x 10⁰

P.

E.

W.

D.

R.

Br. 2
10⁰ x 12⁰

OPTIONAL DEN

COVERED STOOP

Gar.
20⁰ x 23⁸

64' - 0"

36' - 0"

© design basics inc.

Total Square Footage: 1398

- the privately located family room boasts tall windows for a clear view of nature

- a back porch makes a great spot to watch the children play in the yard

- a snack bar easily accommodates a buffet meal

- dinette expands for larger groups

6729-9G SEDGEWICK

PRICE CODE 14

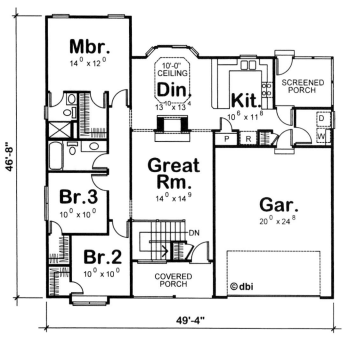

NOTE: 9 FT. MAIN LEVEL WALLS

Total Square Footage: 1406

- open family room shares see-thru fireplace with spacious bayed dinette

- kitchen enjoys wrapping counters, roomy snack bar, pantry and access to a private, screened porch

- laundry room just inside the garage offers a convenient spot for umbrellas and muddy shoes

- master and secondary bedrooms are equipped with walk-in closets

8129-9G CEDAR FALLS

PRICE CODE 14

Total Square Footage: 1420 Optional Finished Basement 994 Sq. Ft.

- two eating areas the dining room open to the great room for entertaining and the breakfast area open to the casual air of the kitchen

- an expansive great room with cathedral ceiling, adds character to conversations there

OPTIONAL FINISHED BASEMENT PLAN INCLUDED

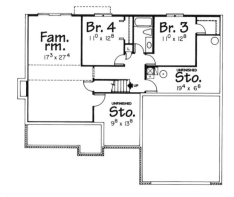

design basics inc.
HOME PLAN DESIGN SERVICE

3010-9G QUIMBY
PRICE CODE 14

Total Square Footage: 1422

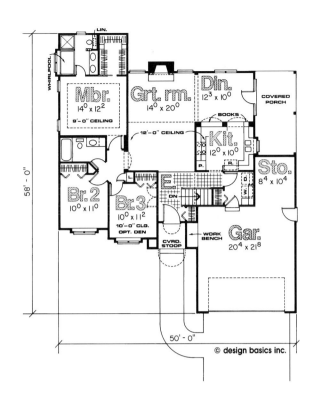

© design basics inc.

- arched openings to kitchen with built-in bookcases provide dramatic backdrop for dining area

- spacious covered porch is accessed from dining room

- garage include space for work bench and sizeable storage area

- master suite features a boxed nine-foot-high ceiling, whirlpool bath and walk-in closet

- 12-foot-tall ceiling integrates great room, semi-formal dining room and kitchen

6728-9G OBERLIN
PRICE CODE 14

NOTE: 9 FT. MAIN LEVEL WALLS

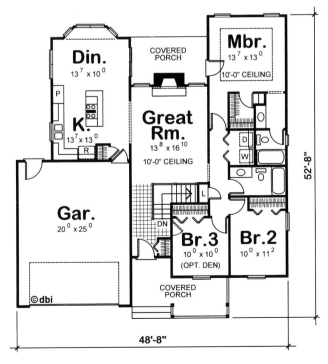

© dbi

Total Square Footage: 1422

- open entry provides pleasing view of the family room with fireplace flanked by windows

- kitchen features coat closet, pantry, center cooktop and snack bar

- sliding doors in the bayed dining area lead to a private covered porch

- luxurious master bedroom enjoys doors to the back porch, a walk-in closet, compartmented bath and convenient access to washer and dryer

www.designbasics.com

25

1379-9G PENDLETON
PRICE CODE 14

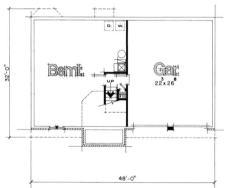

Total Square Footage: 1429

- formal dining room opens to large entry with coat closet and wide stairs

- core hallway opens to large master bedroom with walk-in closet and private bath

- double L-shaped kitchen features boxed window at sink, pantry, and buffet counter

8089-9G CHANDLER HILLS
PRICE CODE 14

Total Square Footage: 1433

- a tall, sloping great room ceiling prompts warm comments from guests who relax there

- arches and columns enhance front porch dedicated to summer

- the master suite is secluded at the rear of the home for peace and quiet

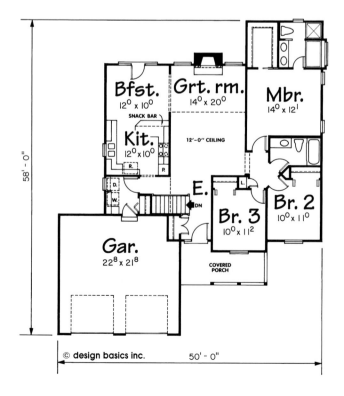

800-947-7526

Total Square Footage: 1437

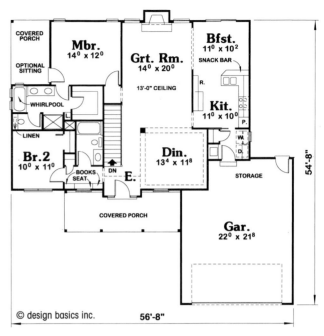

© design basics inc.   56'-8"

NOTE: 9 FT. MAIN LEVEL WALLS

- the master suite offers the retreat options of an outdoor adjacent covered porch or a sitting room

- three windows accent the whirlpool tub in the master bath and are a welcome natural light source for the dual-sink vanity

- built-in bookshelves and a window seat just off the entry help create interest when entering bedroom 2

- a dropped soffit creates a unique perimeter defining the dining room, which easily interacts with the great room when entertaining

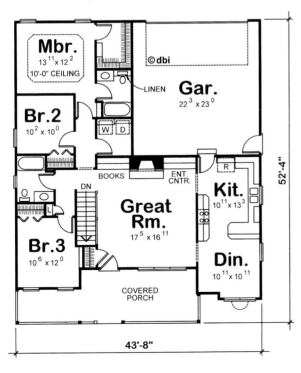

NOTE: 9 FT. MAIN LEVEL WALLS

Total Square Footage: 1446

- a raised hearth fireplace and built-in bookcase and entertainment center provide style and convenience in the open family room

- kitchen features wrapping counters and shares a snack bar with adjoining dinette

- master suite includes roomy walk-in closet, corner windows, boxed ceiling and full bath

- laundry room is centrally located among all three bedrooms

8160-9G BRADFORD POINTE

PRICE CODE 14

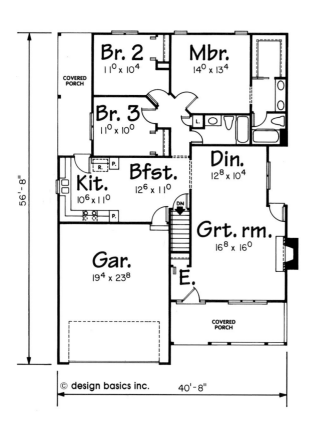

Total Square Footage: 1449

- two porches provide the perfect spot for sipping summertime drinks
- bedroom wing is secluded, providing quiet places to retire to
- daily traffic is inhibited with open living areas

2173-9G FRASER

PRICE CODE 14

Total Square Footage: 1451

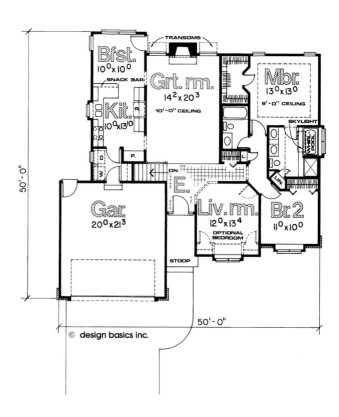

- snack bar and generous pantry in kitchen adjacent to pleasant dinette
- hanging space and cabinet in convenient laundry room access from garage entry
- master bath features his-and-her lavs and whirlpool tub under skylight
- versatility with living room/bedroom option

800-947-7526

8090-9G   SPRING VALLEY

PRICE CODE 14

Total Square Footage: 1453

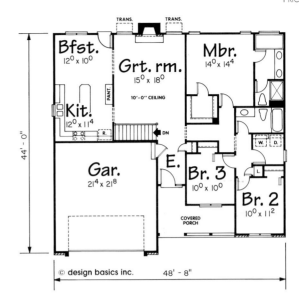

Bfst. 12⁰ x 10⁰
Grt. rm. 15⁰ x 18⁰   10'-0" CEILING
Mbr. 14⁰ x 14⁴
Kit. 12⁰ x 11⁴
Gar. 21⁴ x 21⁸
Br. 3 10⁰ x 10⁰
Br. 2 10⁰ x 11²
COVERED PORCH
44' - 0"
48' - 8"
© design basics inc.

- an island counter adds space to prepare and cook meals

- a front covered porch offers a spot to escape and dream

- a large dinette is open to both formal and informal eating

- a master bedroom has the option of a second closet if needed

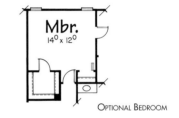

Mbr. 14⁰ x 12⁰

OPTIONAL BEDROOM

5034-9G   PAYSON

PRICE CODE 14

Bfst. 13⁰ x 10⁰
Fam. Rm. 15⁰ x 17⁹   10'-0" CEILING
Mbr. 14⁰ x 14⁴
Kit. 13⁰ x 11⁴
Gar. 21⁴ x 22⁸
Den 10⁰ x 12⁰
WHIRLPOOL
COVERED STOOP
E.
45'-0"
49'-8"
© design basics inc.

NOTE: 9 FT. MAIN LEVEL WALLS

OPTIONAL FINISHED BASEMENT PLAN INCLUDED

Fam. Rm. 35⁷ x 17⁶
ENTERTAINMENT CENTER
Br. 2 12⁰ x 12¹⁰
Kit. 10¹⁰ x 11⁰
Storage
Br. 3 12⁰ x 12¹⁰
SEAT

Total Square Footage: 1472 Optional Finished Basement 1169 Sq. Ft.

- traffic flows neatly through the den just inside the entry

- with no wasted space, the kitchen and breakfast area function as a large living area organized with an island counter

- his-and-her walk-in closets offer plenty of practical storage options in the master suite

- an optional finished basement provides the possibility of creating an apartment for live-in relative

www.designbasics.com

29

3260-9G KIRBY

PRICE CODE 14

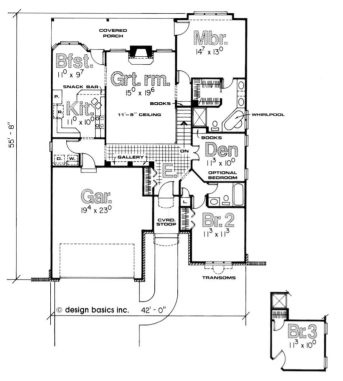

Total Square Footage: 1478

OPTIONAL BEDROOM

- breakfast area provides access to rear covered porch

- master suite features access to covered porch, walk-in closet and corner whirlpool

- private den easily converts to optional bedroom

- gallery wall in entry has artistic appeal

3019-9G KELSEY

PRICE CODE 14

Total Square Footage: 1479

- bowed breakfast area open to kitchen including island snack bar corner sink and access to back yard

- covered porch adds charm to this ranch home

- sunny great room with 11-foot ceiling open to entry

- den with 10-foot-high ceiling and French doors options as a third bedroom

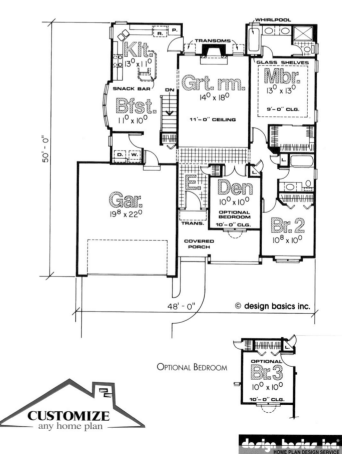

OPTIONAL BEDROOM

CUSTOMIZE
any home plan

design basics inc.
HOME PLAN DESIGN SERVICE

Total Square Footage: 1486

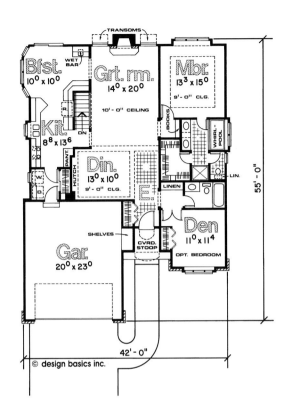

- plan features optional bedroom or private den accessed by French doors

- dinette surrounds you with natural light with its bayed windows and patio door

- sunny master bedroom boasts nine-foot ceiling and built-in bookcase

- master bath has dual vanities, large walk-in closet and oversized whirlpool

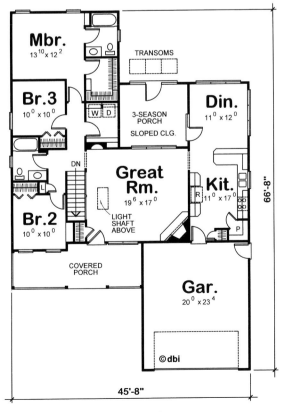

NOTE: 9 FT. MAIN LEVEL WALLS

Total Square Footage: 1495

- family room enjoys decorative stair railing, display alcove, skylight and a built-in entertainment center above the fireplace

- roomy kitchen boasts corner pantry, access from the garage and ample snack bar

- a door in the sunny dining area leads to a stylish three-season porch

- master retreat includes generous walk-in closet, full bath and close proximity to the laundry room

6734-9G KENTON

PRICE CODE 14

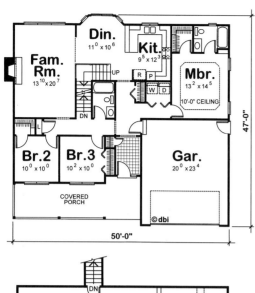

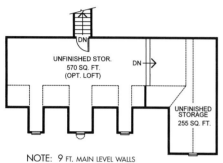

NOTE: 9 FT. MAIN LEVEL WALLS

Total Square Footage: 1495 Unfinished Storage 825 Sq. Ft.

- secluded entry maintains privacy in the rest of the home

- an open stair rail visually expands the bayed dinette area where a roomy snack bar provides extra dining options

- kitchen amenities include wrapping counters, window over the sink and a full size pantry

- spacious family room enjoys triple-wide window and raised hearth fireplace

2300-9G ADAIR

PRICE CODE 14

Total Square Footage: 1496

- luxurious master suite enjoys sunlit whirlpool, dual-lav dressing area and roomy walk-in closet

- tiled entry views spacious great room with window-framed fireplace

- dining area strategic to great room enhances formal or family gatherings

- kitchen/breakfast area is designed for enjoyment and has utility room nearby

- convenient wet bar/servery serves both kitchen and dining area

- bedroom 3 designed for optional conversion to a den or home office

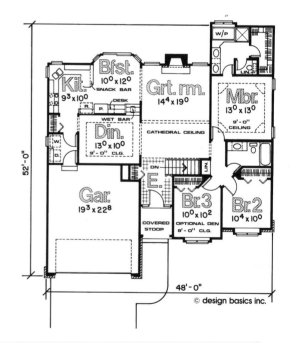

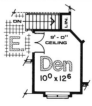

OPTIONAL DEN

design basics inc.
HOME PLAN DESIGN SERVICE

Total Square Footage: 1498

Call us for more
ADA Designs.

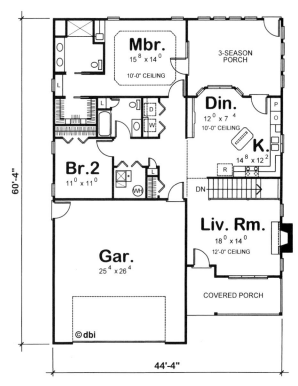

60'-4"

44'-4"

NOTE: 9 FT. MAIN LEVEL WALLS

- this universal design features three-foot doors and wide hallways, extra open areas if baths and a main floor mechanical closet

- special conveniences in the kitchen include wide, shallow pantry, center work island and access to a three-season porch

- the master suite includes a kitchenette, roll-in shower and a door to the porch

- a laundry closet is conveniently located next to the master bedroom

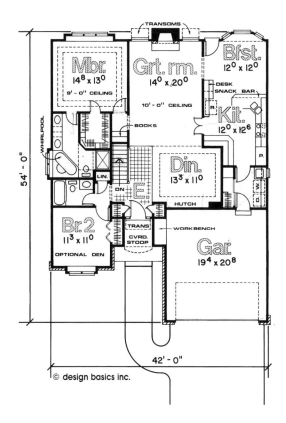

© design basics inc.

42' - 0"

54' - 0"

Total Square Footage: 1499

- master suite features deluxe bath with sloped ceiling and plant shelves above an open shower

- optional den/bedroom provides design flexibility

- garage features built-in workbench

- double doors from great room offer privacy from kitchen

- dinette, featuring desk and snack bar also provides convenient access to outdoors

www.designbasics.com

33

6724-9G BEHRENS

PRICE CODE 14

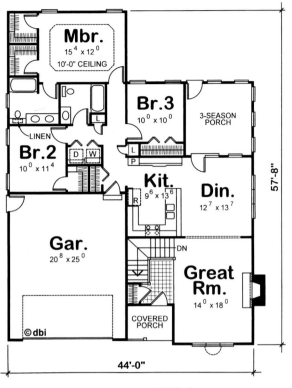

Mbr.
15⁴ x 12⁰
10'-0" CEILING

Br.3
10⁰ x 10⁰

3-SEASON PORCH

LINEN

Br.2
10⁰ x 11⁴

Kit.
9⁶ x 13⁶

Din.
12⁷ x 13⁷

Gar.
20⁸ x 25⁰

57'-8"

DN

Great Rm.
14⁰ x 18⁰

COVERED PORCH

©dbi

44'-0"

NOTE: 9 FT. MAIN LEVEL WALLS

Total Square Footage: 1506

- an arch-topped triple-wide window provides a stunning focal point to this open family room with fireplace and lovely adjoining entry

- combined kitchen and dinette offer wall-length pantry, roomy snack bar and access to a charming three-season porch

- special amenities in the master suite include corner windows, boxed ceiling his-and-her walk-in closets and double vanities

- laundry closet is conveniently located near bedrooms

6271-9G TORRINGTON

PRICE CODE 15

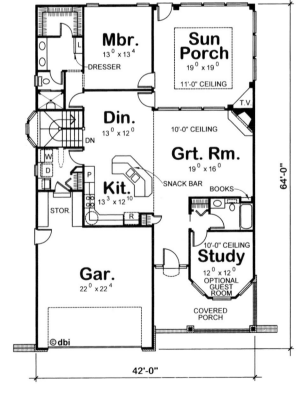

Mbr.
13⁰ x 13⁴
DRESSER

Sun Porch
19⁰ x 19⁰
11'-0" CEILING

T.V.

Din.
13⁰ x 12⁰

DN

10'-0" CEILING

Grt. Rm.
19⁰ x 16⁰

64'-0"

W
D

P

Kit.
13³ x 12¹⁰

SNACK BAR

BOOKS

STOR.

R

10'-0" CEILING

Study
12⁰ x 12⁰
OPTIONAL GUEST ROOM

Gar.
22⁰ x 22⁴

©dbi

COVERED PORCH

42'-0"

Total Square Footage: 1509

- transom-topped bay windows enhance the den which easily doubles as a guest room with a bathroom nearby

- garage offers extra storage in the back as well as pull down stairs to utilize space above

- open great room enjoys 10-foot ceiling, corner fireplace and ample windows combined kitchen/nook feature a pantry, lazy Susan, angled snack bar and access to lovely sun porch

- master suite amenities include compartmented bath, double vanity, built-in dresser and walk-in closet

NOTE: 9 FT. MAIN LEVEL WALLS

design basics inc.
HOME PLAN DESIGN SERVICE

Total Square Footage: 1511

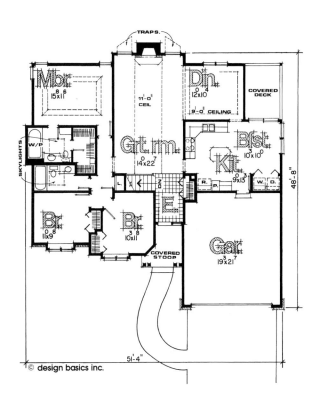

© design basics inc.

51'-4"

48'-8"

- dramatic high entry framed by columns and windows

- expansive great room features sloped ceilings to 11-feet and impressive fireplace surrounded by windows

- formal ceiling in dining room

- complete island kitchen includes lazy Susan, pantry and desk plus adjacent laundry area

- master bath features skylight and walk-in closet

8015-9G COPPER CREEK
PRICE CODE 15

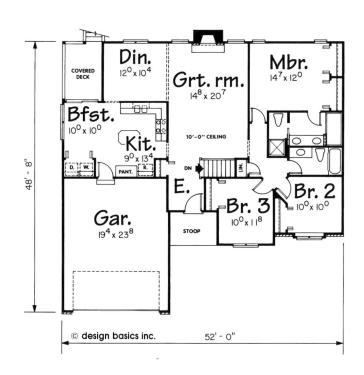

© design basics inc.   52'-0"

48'-8"

Total Square Footage: 1515

- a large dining and great room are located next to each other - perfect for parties

- an organized kitchen easily accesses the garage and dinette

- a rear covered deck communes with nature

- two secondary bedrooms accommodate overnight family and guests

6265-9G EDINBOROUGH

PRICE CODE 15

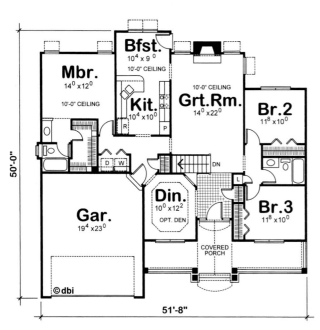

Mbr.
14⁰ x 12⁰

10'-0" CEILING

Bfst.
10⁴ x 9⁰

10'-0" CEILING

Kit.
10⁴ x 10⁰

Grt.Rm.
14⁰ x 22⁰

10'-0" CEILING

Br.2
11⁸ x 10⁰

Din.
10⁰ x 12²

OPT. DEN

Br.3
11⁸ x 10⁰

Gar.
19⁴ x 23⁰

©dbi

50'-0"

51'-8"

COVERED PORCH

DN

NOTE: 9 FT. MAIN LEVEL WALLS

CUSTOMIZE
any home plan

Total Square Footage: 1517

• special angles and ceiling detail enhance the dining room which easily converts to a den

• spacious great room enjoys 10-foot ceiling, transom-topped windows, fireplace and open staircase

• wrapping counters, a pantry and snack bar add convenience in the kitchen

• transom-topped windows, a 10-foot ceiling, compartmented bath and walk-in closet highlight the master suite

3555-9G LARAMY

PRICE CODE 15

Total Square Footage: 1518

• cathedral ceiling adds drama to family room with fireplace framed by windows

• volume entry is adorned with arched transom above door

• covered porch off breakfast area welcomes relaxation

• spacious walk-in closet, whirlpool under window and dual sink vanity serve master bath

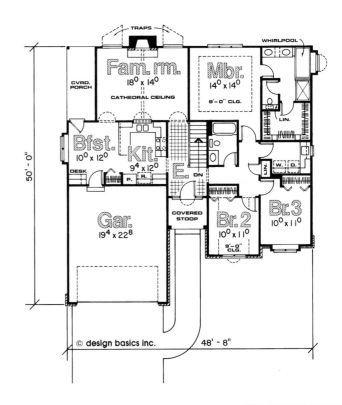

TRAPS

Fam. rm.
18⁰ x 14⁰

CATHEDRAL CEILING

Mbr.
14⁰ x 14⁰

9'-0" CLG.

WHIRLPOOL

CVRD. PORCH

LIN.

Bfst.
10⁰ x 12⁰

DESK

Kit.
9⁴ x 12⁰

P.

R.

DN

LIN.

W. D.

Gar.
19⁴ x 22⁸

COVERED STOOP

Br. 2
10⁰ x 11⁰

9'-0" CLG.

Br.3
10⁰ x 11⁰

50' - 0"

© design basics inc.

48' - 8"

design basics inc.

HOME PLAN DESIGN SERVICE

Total Square Footage: 1520

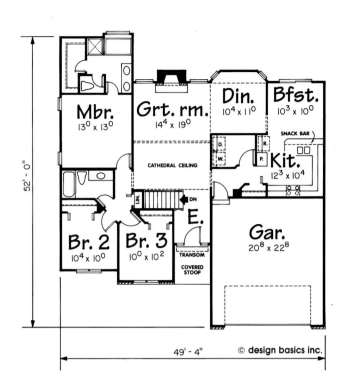

Mbr.
13^0 x 13^0

Grt. rm.
14^4 x 19^0

CATHEDRAL CEILING

Din.
10^4 x 11^0

Bfst.
10^3 x 10^0

SNACK BAR

Kit.
12^3 x 10^4

Br. 2
10^4 x 10^0

Br. 3
10^0 x 10^2

E.

TRANSOM

COVERED STOOP

Gar.
20^8 x 22^8

LIN.

DN

52' - 0"

49' - 4"

© design basics inc.

• great room enjoys sloped ceiling and warmth of a crackling fireplace

• patio doors in the breakfast area leading to backyard fun and bring in sunshine

• bayed dining room windows add definition to memories created there

---

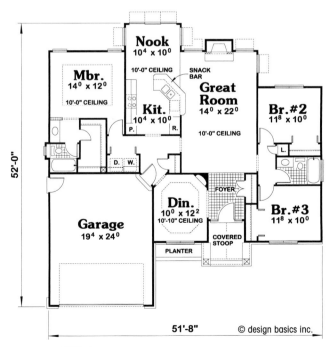

Nook
10^4 x 10^0

10'-0" CEILING

SNACK BAR

Mbr.
14^0 x 12^0

10'-0" CEILING

Kit.
10^4 x 10^0

Great Room
14^0 x 22^0

10'-0" CEILING

Br.#2
11^8 x 10^0

D. W.

Garage
19^4 x 24^0

Din.
10^0 x 12^2

10'-10" CEILING

FOYER

COVERED STOOP

PLANTER

Br.#3
11^8 x 10^0

52'-0"

51'-8"

© design basics inc.

NOTE: 9 FT. MAIN LEVEL WALLS

Total Square Footage: 1528

• the kitchen opens itself up to the nook and great room - both of which have access to its large snack bar

• the master bedroom has a 10-foot-high boxed ceiling and a generous walk-in closet

• stacked stone and stucco combine with clay tile to give the home a Southwest feel

• the split floor plan allows the master bedroom to have more privacy

www.designbasics.com

24029-9G FELDON

PRICE CODE 15

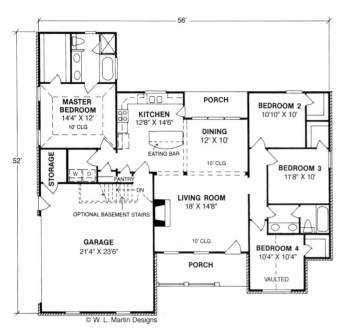

© W. L. Martin Designs

Total Square Footage: 1539

CUSTOMIZE
any home plan

- 10-foot celings add a sense of spaciousness to the living and dining rooms

- cabinets wrap around a central island with eating bar in the kitchen

- the garage offers a walk-in storage closet

- those in the master suite will enjoy its walk-in closet, soaking tub and double vanity

- a compartmented bath serves the three additional bedrooms, allowing more than one to get ready

24051-9G CABRIE

PRICE CODE 15

Total Square Footage: 1541

- the living room provides two window views, a corner fireplace and entertainment wall

- those in the dining room won't miss any activity in the living room and can access the rear porch

- the master suite, with soaking bath and walk-in closet, has a direct connection to the laundry room

- a work bench will be a welcome feature in the garage

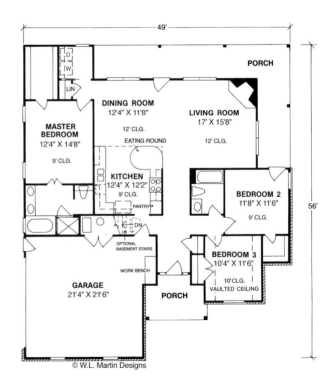

© W.L. Martin Designs

design basics inc
HOME PLAN DESIGN SERVICE

Total Square Footage: 1552

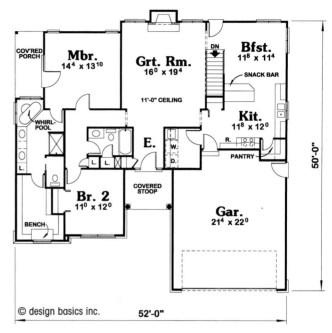

NOTE: 9 FT. MAIN LEVEL WALLS

- the master suite is a haven for time alone with its own covered porch, corner whirlpool tub and large shower

- 11-foot high ceilings in the entry and great room bring a sense of airiness

- linen closets in both the master bath accomodate a place for toiletries

- a separate laundry room keeps clothes from view and has space for an ironing board

- a corner walk-in pantry, utility closet, and snack bar help organize the wide kitchen

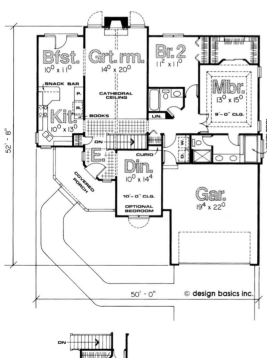

OPTIONAL BEDROOM

Total Square Footage: 1554

- entry open to great room with cathedral ceiling and formal dining room with 10-foot-high ceiling

- spacious kitchen features corner sink, built-in bookcase and shares snack bar with breakfast area

- French doors open to master suite with volume ceiling, mirrored doors to walk-in closet and sunny whirlpool bath

www.designbasics.com

1770-9G BAYLEY

PRICE CODE 15

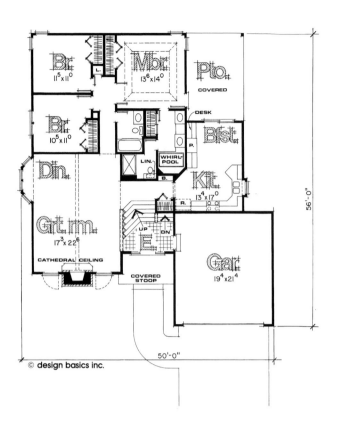

© design basics inc.

Total Square Footage: 1556

- large great room with cathedral ceiling features fireplace framed by beautiful windows

- large master suite with his and her closets, whirlpool, two lavs with make-up counter and private access to covered deck

- bayed dining area open to great room for expanded entertaining

- efficient kitchen with pantry, desk and sunny dinette leading to covered patio

5460-9G SULLIVAN

PRICE CODE 15

Total Square Footage: 1558

- a raised-hearth fireplace and built-in entertainment center do not deter the view in the great room

- a sloped ceiling enhances the master bath with romantic, corner whirlpool tub

- bedroom 2 features plenty of separation from the master suite and has access to its own full bath and linen closet

- a separate laundry room hosts a soaking sink and hanging closet

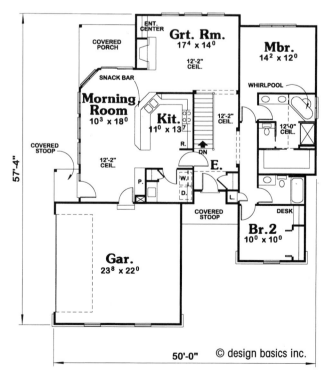

© design basics inc.

NOTE: 9 FT. MAIN LEVEL WALLS

Total Square Footage: 1561

© design basics inc.

- breakfast area has built-in desk and access to covered deck or great room

- volume entry offers view of great room fireplace

- flexible dining area and great room share 10-foot ceiling

- formal living room converts to optional third bedroom

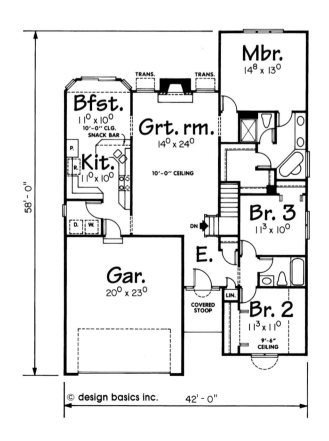

© design basics inc.   42'- 0"

Total Square Footage: 1562

- a large great room provides plenty of space when the family comes home

- two secondary bedrooms can be used as sleeping areas or places to explore a hobby

- traffic from garage to kitchen is streamlined for un-loading the car after grocery shopping

6735-9G COVENTRY

PRICE CODE 15

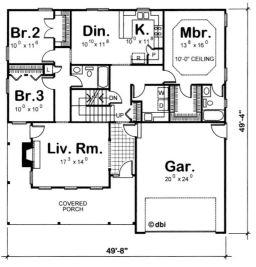

NOTE: 9 FT. MAIN LEVEL WALLS

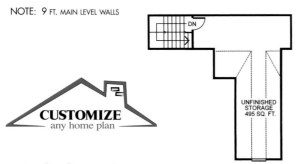

CUSTOMIZE any home plan

Total Square Footage: 1570 Unfinished Storage 495 Sq. Ft.

- ample windows on two sides, a charming fireplace and a door leading to the wrap-around porch highlight this family room

- separated from the master suite, secondary bedrooms are equipped with generous closets and share a full bath

- a combined kitchen and dining room feature wrapping counters, large snack bar and patio doors to the back yard

- special ceiling detail and corner windows enhance the master bedroom which comes with full bath and large walk-in closet

5457-9G ASHCROFT

PRICE CODE 15

Total Square Footage: 1577

- a large walk-in closet provides plenty of wardrobe space for the master suite

- guests will have complete privacy in bedroom 2 with its own full bath and walk-in closet

- oak flooring throughout all living areas creates visual integration among all rooms

- a large pantry accompanies the kitchen with angled snack bar

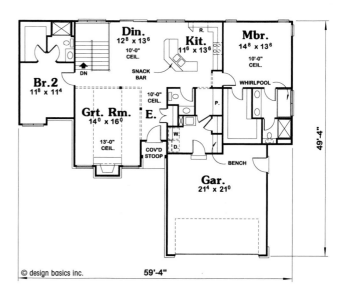

NOTE: 9 FT. MAIN LEVEL WALLS

800-947-7526

design basics inc
HOME PLAN DESIGN SERVICE

Total Square Footage: 1577

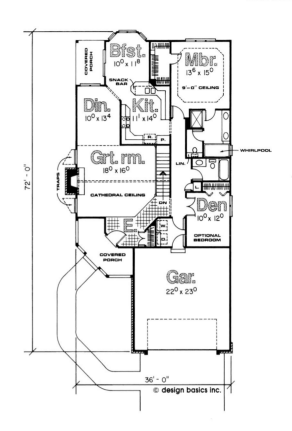

- generous master bedroom offers nine-foot-high boxed ceiling, walk-in closet and whirlpool with window

- angled entry with covered porch adds interest to this exciting one-story design

- private, covered rear patio accessed from dinette

- raised-hearth fireplace centered under cathedral ceiling in expansive great room

- well-equipped kitchen with snack bar easily accesses bayed dinette and formal dining room

8087-9G COLLINS FALLS
PRICE CODE 15

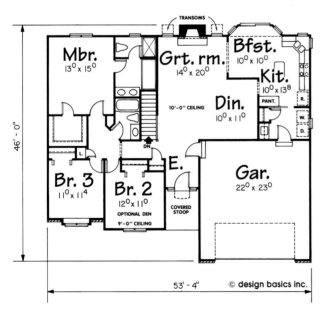

OPTIONAL DEN

Total Square Footage: 1579

- a dining room becomes expandable space for the great room and vice-versa

- a bayed breakfast area offers plenty of sunlight for cooking and eating

- a third bedroom is flexible as a den for those who need an office or a quiet place to wind down

2537-9G TAHOE

PRICE CODE 15

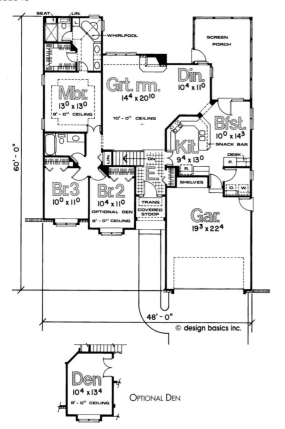

© design basics inc.

Total Square Footage: 1580

OPTIONAL DEN

- dining room opens to great room, offering view of fireplace

- kitchen features large pantry, planning desk and snack bar

- dinette accesses large, comfortable screen porch

- laundry room is strategically located off kitchen and provides direct access from garage

- French doors access master suite with formal ceiling and pampering bath

2324-9G OAKRIDGE

PRICE CODE 15

Total Square Footage: 1583

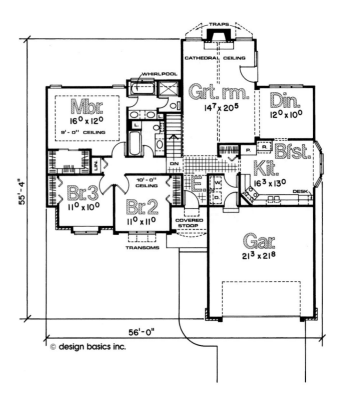

© design basics inc.

- cathedral ceiling and fireplace flanked by trapezoid windows highlight great room

- expansive great room, dining room, sunny kitchen/breakfast area encourage leisure and entertaining pursuits

- compartmented bath features window to flood whirlpool and vanity/makeup area with natural light

- striking 10-foot-high entry has plant shelf integrated above closet

design basics inc.
HOME PLAN DESIGN SERVICE

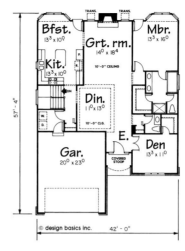

Total Square Footage: 1593 Optional Finished Basement 1137 Sq. Ft.

OPTIONAL
FINISHED BASEMENT
PLAN INCLUDED

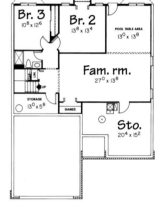

- an optional walk-out basement pro- vides extra bedrooms, storage and living space

- a spacious island kitchen includes wrapping counters and a pantry

- an open entertaining area is versatile for holidays and gatherings

3578-9G STONYBROOK
PRICE CODE 15

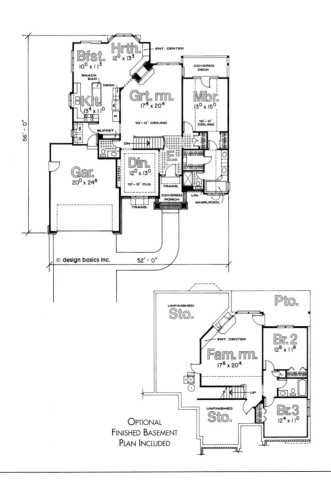

Total Square Footage: 1595 Optional Finished Basement 790 Sq. Ft.

OPTIONAL
FINISHED BASEMENT
PLAN INCLUDED

- great room features 10-foot ceiling and angled see-thru fireplace

- kitchen accommodates boxed window over sink, planning desk and island counter

- master bedroom overlooks private, covered deck

- optional finished basement has plans for additional bedrooms and family room

www.designbasics.com

45

1017-9G KIRWIN

PRICE CODE 15

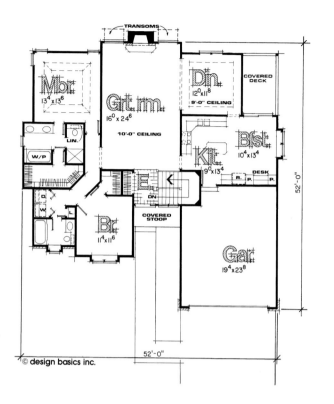

Total Square Footage: 1598

- efficient island kitchen features two pantries, lazy Susan, planning desk and sunny breakfast area accessing covered deck

- main floor laundry room conveniently located near bedrooms

- formal dining room open to great room

- master dressing/bath area complete with double vanity, large walk-in closet and whirlpool tub

- angled hallway offers privacy to guest bedroom and hall bath

2291-9G BRADLEY

PRICE CODE 15

Total Square Footage: 1599

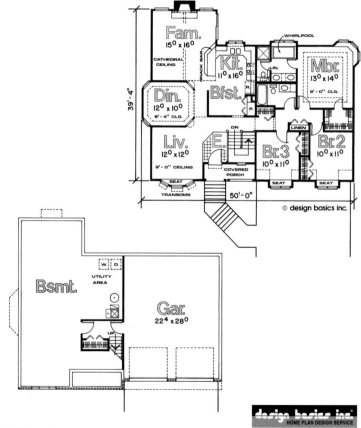

- entry opens to living room with cozy bayed window with a built-in seat

- family room opens to kitchen and has cozy fireplace and cathedral ceiling

- well-designed kitchen/breakfast area with wrapping counters and snack bar

- natural light from a bayed window floods the charming master suite

design basics inc.
HOME PLAN DESIGN SERVICE

Total Square Footage: 1604

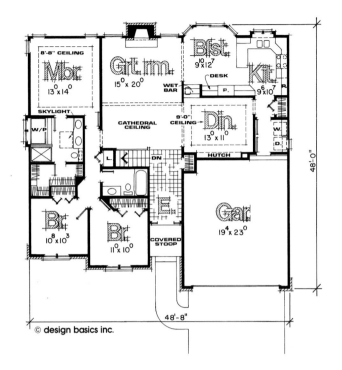

© design basics inc.

- large volume great room with fire-place flanked by windows to the back seen from entry

- fully-equipped kitchen with desk, pantry and special window box above sink

- extra deep garage

- roomy master suite with volume ceiling equipped with special amenities including skylit dressing/bath area with plant shelf, large walk-in closet, double vanity and whirlpool tub

- see-thru wet bar between dinette and dining room with formal ceiling

2923-9G SUTTON
PRICE CODE 16

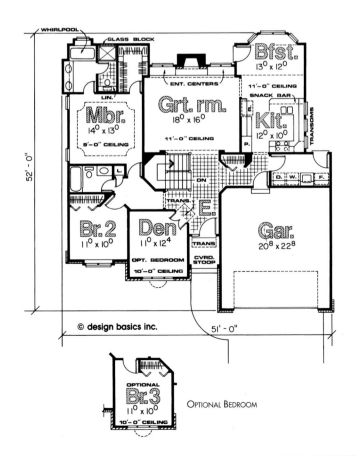

© design basics inc.

OPTIONAL Bedroom

Total Square Footage: 1622

- U-shaped stairs form beautiful focal point between 10-foot-tall entry and large great room with brick fireplace between built-in entertainment centers

- den with angled French doors off entry is optional bedroom 3

- master suite features nice ceiling detail, sunny whirlpool bath, glass block at shower and generous walk-in closet

www.designbasics.com

47

8080-9G MAPLE GROVE

PRICE CODE 16

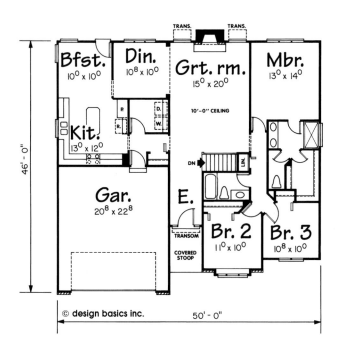

Total Square Footage: 1628

CUSTOMIZE
any home plan

- an island counter in the kitchen makes cooking and serving more convenient

- formal and informal eating are located near each other, for extra space when larger groups stay to eat

- master suite enjoys large walk-in closet, compartmented bath and double vanity

8079-9G BELLE HARBOR

PRICE CODE 16

Total Square Footage: 1633

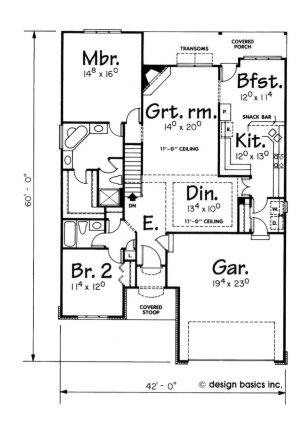

- 11-foot ceilings enhance the entry, dining room and great room

- a long back porch offers a lazy welcome to the outdoors

- the master bath enjoys his and her vanities and a corner soaking tub for a feeling of luxury

5466-9G SOMERDALE
PRICE CODE 16

Total Square Footage: 1636

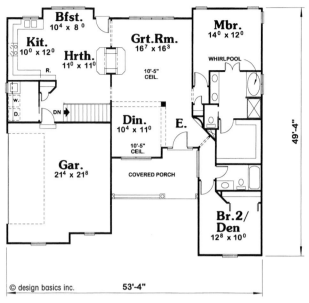

Bfst.
10^4 x 8^0

Kit.
10^0 x 12^0

Hrth.
11^0 x 11^0

R.

W.
D.

DN

Gar.
21^4 x 21^8

Grt.Rm.
16^7 x 16^3

10'-5"
CEIL.

Din.
10^4 x 11^0

10'-5"
CEIL.

COVERED PORCH

E.

Mbr.
14^0 x 12^0

WHIRLPOOL

49'-4"

Br.2/ Den
12^8 x 10^0

© design basics inc.   53'-4"

NOTE: 9 FT. MAIN LEVEL WALLS

- an informal atmosphere was designed in the kitchen with space shared by a hearth room and dinette

- accompanying the master bedroom, French doors open to a full bath with large vanity, whirlpool and spacious walk-in closet

- a see-thru fireplace offers its casual ambiance to all living areas of this home

- guests can easily mingle between the open design of the dining room and great room

2377-9G LEIGHTON
PRICE CODE 16

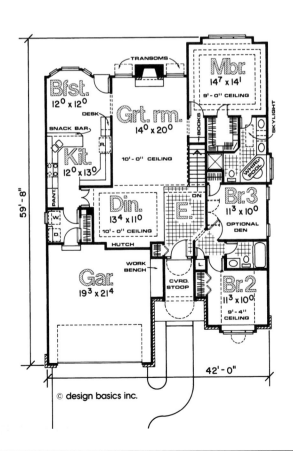

TRANSOMS

Bfst.
12^0 x 12^0

DESK

SNACK BAR

Kit.
12^0 x 13^0

PANT.

Grt. rm.
14^0 x 20^0

10'- 0" CEILING

Mbr.
14^7 x 14^1
9'- 0" CEILING

SKYLIGHT

BOOKS

WHIRLPOOL

Din.
13^4 x 11^0
10'- 0" CEILING

HUTCH

Br.3
11^3 x 10^0

OPTIONAL DEN

E

DN

W.
D.

Gar.
19^3 x 21^4

WORK BENCH

CVRD. STOOP

L

Br.2
11^3 x 10^0
9'- 4" CEILING

59'- 8"

42'- 0"

© design basics inc.

Total Square Footage: 1636

- great room features cozy fireplace flanked by bright windows

- gourmet kitchen and bayed dinette includes snack bar wrapping counters, planning desk and access to outdoors

- secondary bedrooms share bath bedroom 3 designed as optional den

- master dressing/bath area includes skylight, his-and-her vanities and corner whirlpool

www.designbasics.com

49

3915-9G ITHACA

PRICE CODE 16

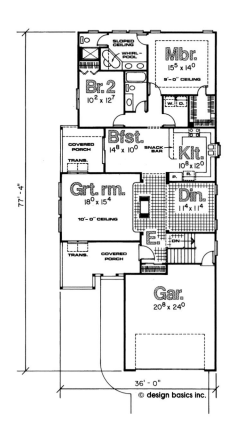

Total Square Footage: 1643

- great room and dining room are both connected and enhanced by openings that flank a see-thru fire place and mantle

- laundry room is located near bedrooms and hall bath for practicality and convenience

- kitchen with two lazy Susans, pantry and snack bar opens to spacious breakfast area with access to covered side porch

- covered porch provides a pleasant focal point on this home's front elevation

5179-9G SPENLOW

PRICE CODE 16

Total Square Footage: 1650

- the dining room room is located within close proximity to the kitchen and is defined with a boxed ceiling

- at 11-feet in height, the great room establishes a haven for welcome and family activity

- accompanying the master bedroom, is a large walk-in closet, whirlpool and dual-lav vanity

- the efficient kitchen is equipped with counter space that's useful when serving formal meals in the dining room

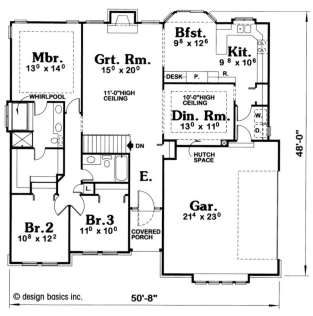

NOTE: 9 FT. MAIN LEVEL WALLS

CUSTOMIZE
any home plan

design basics inc.
HOME PLAN DESIGN SERVICE

Total Square Footage: 1651

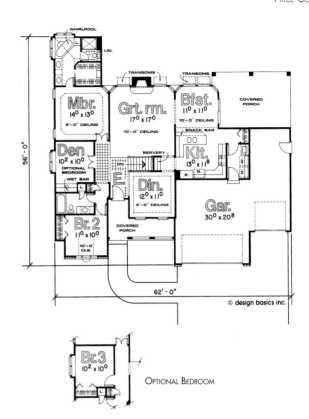

OPTIONAL BEDROOM

- covered front porch with wood railing combines with covered rear porch to expand living space outside

- bright, bayed breakfast area offers access to covered porch

- den with wet bar enhances privacy of master suite or can be converted to optional third bedroom

Total Square Footage: 1653

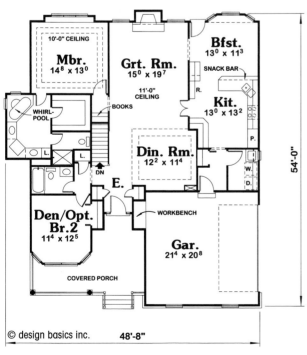

NOTE: 9 FT. MAIN LEVEL WALLS

- a front porch reminiscent of the 1920s sets the tone on this charming one-story home

- the spacious kitchen and dinette facilitate good circulation for daily use

- plenty of extra space in the master bath leaves room to fully utilize the corner make-up counter and his-and-her vanities

- a built-in workbench in the garage provides a place for tools

2907-9G ASHLEY

PRICE CODE 16

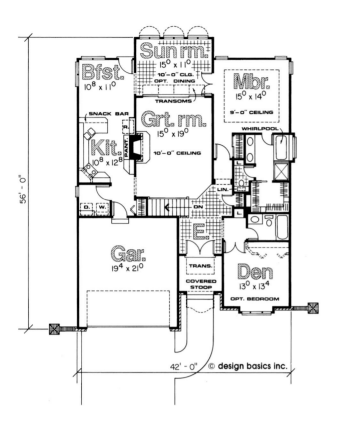

Total Square Footage: 1658

- entry captures fantastic views from great room to sun room with arched windows

- peninsula kitchen featuring corner sink and snack bar is open to breakfast area

- den off entry has bedroom option

- sun room offers access to breakfast area, great room and master suite or can option as a lovely dining room

- spacious master suite includes whirlpool bath with dual-lavs and walk-in closet

5080-9G THOMASTON

PRICE CODE 16

Total Square Footage: 1660

- traditional styling can be found in this home's mouldings, cornerboards and double-hung windows

- a large walk-in closet, whirlpool, and dual-lav vanity assist getting ready in the master bath

- the dining room could easily convert into a family computer/homework area

- a pocket door encloses the laundry room, which includes a back closet and soaking sink

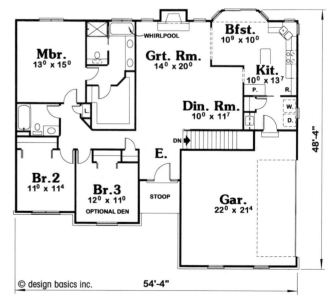

NOTE: 9 FT. MAIN LEVEL WALLS

OPTIONAL DEN

6804-9G Tucson

PRICE CODE 16

Total Square Footage: 1666

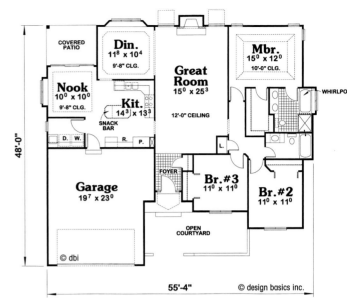

NOTE: 9 FT. MAIN LEVEL WALLS

CUSTOMIZE
any home plan

- a 12-foot ceiling and tall transom-topped windows flanking the fire-place make this large great room seem even bigger

- amenities in the master suite include a vaulted ceiling, corner windows, walk-in closet, dual vanity and whirlpool

- an open kitchen with center work island and snack bar provides easy access to formal dining room and nook

- a boxed window, trayed ceiling and nine-foot sliding doors to a covered patio highlight the nook

2290-9G Monterey

PRICE CODE 16

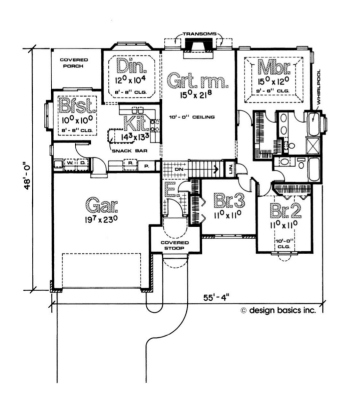

Total Square Footage: 1666

- inviting entry with view into great room is enhanced by arched window and plant shelves above

- bayed window dining room nestled between great room and superb kitchen/breakfast area

- fireplace in great room framed by sunny windows with transoms above

- peaceful master suite enjoys vaulted ceiling, roomy walk-in closet and sunlit master bath with dual-lavs and whirlpool

www.designbasics.com

53

5177-9G CEDRIC

PRICE CODE 16

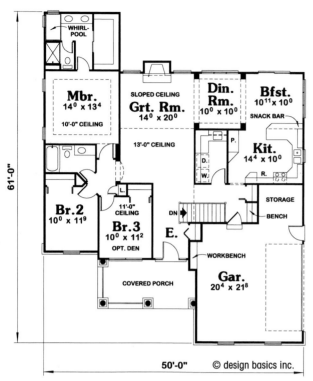

61'-0"

50'-0"   © design basics inc.

NOTE: 9 FT. MAIN LEVEL WALLS

WHIRL-POOL

Mbr.
14⁰ x 13⁴
10'-0" CEILING

SLOPED CEILING
Grt. Rm.
14⁰ x 20⁰
13'-0" CEILING

Din. Rm.
10⁰ x 10⁰

Bfst.
10¹¹ x 10⁰
SNACK BAR

P.

Kit.
14⁴ x 10⁰

D.
W.

R.

Br. 2
10⁰ x 11⁹

11'-0" CEILING

Br. 3
10⁰ x 11²
OPT. DEN

E.

DN

STORAGE

BENCH

WORKBENCH

COVERED PORCH

Gar.
20⁴ x 21⁸

Total Square Footage: 1679

- brick pedestals anchoring tapered columns and a detailed entablature provide the framework of this nostalgic front porch

- bedroom 3 could easily become a den with double doors opening to the entry

- extra counter area in the laundry room extends its available working space

- both the dining room and breakfast area are near the kitchen and readily expand into one another

- a boxed ceiling offers beauty in the master bedroom which also features a large walk-in closet and whirlpool tub

3889-9G MONTCLARE

PRICE CODE 16

Total Square Footage: 1684

- arched brick detailing and columns at the covered stoop provide a refined air to the elevation

- island kitchen adjoins spacious breakfast area with access to outdoors

- master suite includes volume of sloped ceiling, skylit dressing area with double vanity, whirlpool tub and walk-in closet

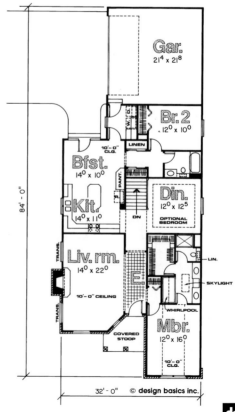

84'-0"

32'-0"   © design basics inc.

Gar.
21⁴ x 21⁸

Br. 2
12⁰ x 10⁰

W.

LINEN

Bfst.
14⁰ x 10⁰
10'-0" CLG.

PANT.

Kit.
14⁰ x 11⁰

DN

Din.
12⁰ x 12⁵

OPTIONAL BEDROOM

Liv. rm.
14⁰ x 22⁰
10'-0" CEILING

TRANS.

TRANS.

E.

LIN.

SKYLIGHT

WHIRLPOOL

COVERED STOOP

Mbr.
12⁰ x 16⁰
10'-0" CLG.

Br. 3
12⁰ x 10¹

OPTIONAL BEDROOM

design basics inc.
HOME PLAN DESIGN SERVICE

Total Square Footage: 1686 Optional Finished Basement 1140 Sq. Ft.

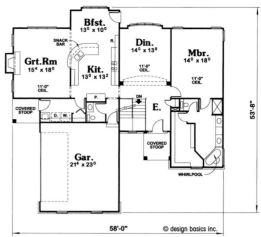

NOTE: 9 FT. MAIN LEVEL WALLS

- the kitchen, dinette and great room were designed for families to interact on a daily basis

- bowed windows and thick columns define the formal dining room

- a long walk-in closet and corner whirlpool give luxury and convenience to the master suite

- in the optional finished basement, a large family room and kitchenette accompany two bedrooms and a full bath

- a soaking sink and closet were included in the laundry room featuring access to a covered stoop

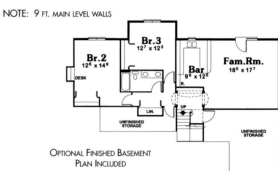

OPTIONAL FINISHED BASEMENT
PLAN INCLUDED

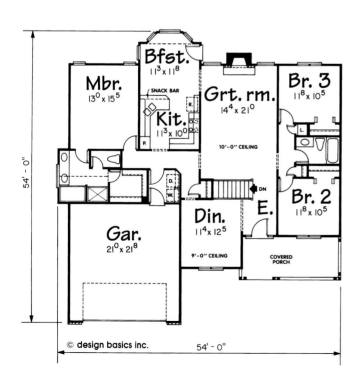

Total Square Footage: 1691

- master suite is separated from secondary bedrooms

- great room offers views of the outdoors or a glowing fireplace

- amenities in the kitchen include wrapping counters, a pantry and a snack bar

24017-9G MARGO
PRICE CODE 16

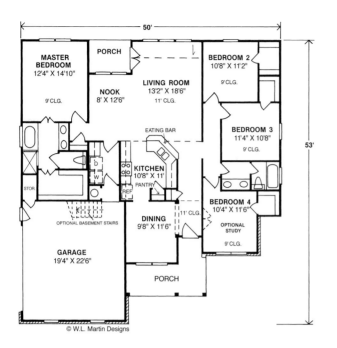

© W.L. Martin Designs

Total Square Footage: 1694

- within steps of the dining room, the kitchen features a pantry and eating bar

- tucked between the breakfast nook and living room, a rear porch offers a place to get away

- if the fourth bedroom isn't needed, it easily converts into a study

- the master suite features French doors that open to a walk-in closet, double vanity and soaking tub

- a walk-in storage closet in the garage is handy for placing tools and lawn equipment

1262-9G COVINGTON
PRICE CODE 16

Total Square Footage: 1696

© design basics inc.

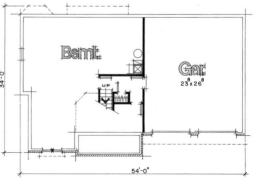

- floor-to-ceiling windows in great room viewed from entry

- main floor laundry room strategically located

- master bath includes whirlpool tub, dual vanity and generous walk-in closet

- efficient double-L kitchen with bayed breakfast area to the back

56 800-947-7526

design basics inc.
HOME PLAN DESIGN SERVICE

Total Square Footage: 1697

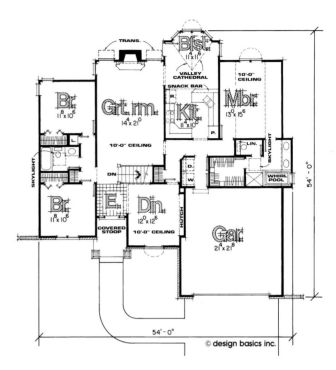

© design basics inc.

- volume dining room with hutch space and elegant arched window open to entry

- expansive great room with 10-foot ceiling offers brick fireplace framed by windows to the back

- kitchen with wrapping counters, snack bar corner sink and pantry

- garage accesses home through conveniently located laundry room

3919-9G DUNBAR
PRICE CODE 16

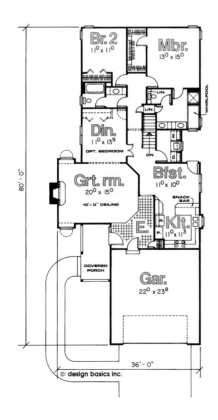

© design basics inc.

Total Square Footage: 1699

- entry provides an expansive view across great room, which freely connects to formal dining room

- kitchen with snack bar, pantry and window sink, adjoins spacious break fast area with access to outdoors

- roomy master suite includes dressing area with double vanity, corner windows and a walk-in closet

- covered front porch shelters side entry and adds charming appeal

www.designbasics.com

8168-9G SONORA SPRINGS
PRICE CODE 17

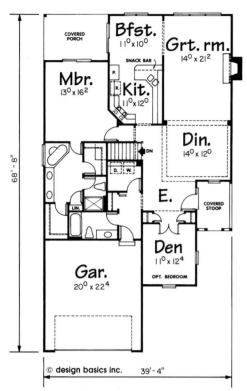

OPTIONAL BEDROOM

Total Square Footage: 1705

- a den with French doors doubles as a bedroom

- a walk-through kitchen provides access to other areas of the main floor

- a back porch adds leisure space to the master bedroom.

- great room and dining room are expandable

8078-9G NORTH CLIFFS
PRICE CODE 17

Total Square Footage: 1707

- back and front covered porches are provided - one for talking with the neighbors and the other for barbeques

- a cathedral ceiling and fireplace enhance the great room

- a snack bar, island counter and extra counter space along one wall make the kitchen more efficient

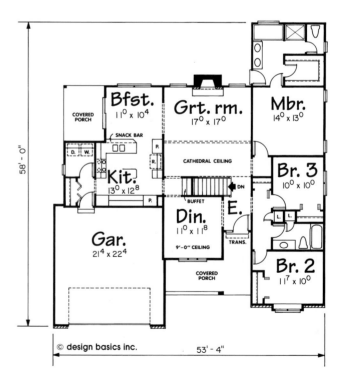

2355-9G WAVERLY

PRICE CODE 17

Total Square Footage: 1710

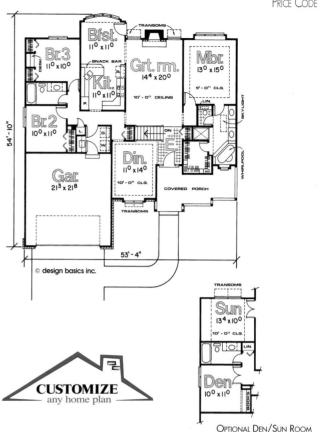

© design basics inc.

- kitchen and dinette area with snack bar, pantry, and access to outdoors

- two secondary bedrooms convertible to a sun room with French doors from the dinette and an optional den

- secluded master suite features boxed ceiling, skylit dressing area, his and her lavs with knee space between, corner whirlpool tub and roomy walk-in closet

CUSTOMIZE
any home plan

OPTIONAL DEN/SUN ROOM

5473-9G WOODRIDGE

PRICE CODE 17

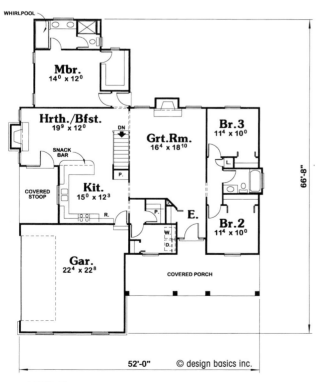

NOTE: 9 FT. MAIN LEVEL WALLS

Total Square Footage: 1712

- a deep front porch makes a great intermediary from the outside to the front entry

- a side porch makes a convenient entry into the home and makes a great area to grill

- a combination breakfast/hearth room is informally integrated with the kitchen

- a walk-in pantry/closet near the laundry room leaves no wasted space in the home

www.designbasics.com

59

8069-9G QUAIL HOLLOW

PRICE CODE 17

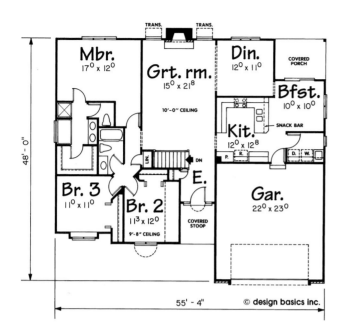

Mbr.
17⁰ x 12⁰

Grt. rm.
15⁰ x 21⁸

10'-0" CEILING

Din.
12⁰ x 11⁰

COVERED PORCH

Bfst.
10⁰ x 10⁰

Kit.
12⁰ x 12⁸

SNACK BAR

Br. 3
11⁰ x 11⁰

Br. 2
11³ x 12⁰

9'-8" CEILING

E.

Gar.
22⁰ x 23⁰

COVERED STOOP

TRANS.   TRANS.

DN

LIN.

P.   R.

D.   W.

48' - 0"

55' - 4"

© design basics inc.

Total Square Footage: 1729

CUSTOMIZE
any home plan

- a snack bar in the kitchen provides the perfect place for one to sit and chat while another bakes

- a great room welcomes hearty discussion

- a back porch offers a quiet place to enjoy a cup of coffee and read the paper

2212-9G SEVILLE

PRICE CODE 17

Total Square Footage: 1735

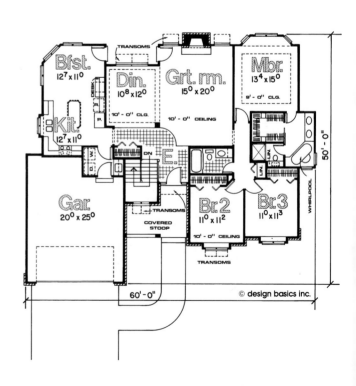

Bfst.
12⁷ x 11⁰

Din.
10⁸ x 12⁰

10'-0" CLG.

Grt. rm.
15⁰ x 20⁰

10'-0" CEILING

Mbr.
13⁴ x 15⁰

9'-0" CLG.

Kit.
12⁷ x 11⁰

DESK

P.

D.   W.

DN

E.

LIN.

LIN.

WHIRLPOOL

Gar.
20⁰ x 25⁰

COVERED STOOP

Br. 2
11⁰ x 11²

Br. 3
11⁰ x 11³

10'-0" CEILING

TRANSOMS

TRANSOMS

TRANSOMS

50' - 0"

60' - 0"

© design basics inc.

- 10-foot-high ceiling for volume in entry, great room and dining room

- dining room open to great room for entertaining options

- extra length in garage for storage

- open staircase with landing for possible finished basement

- angled whirlpool, double vanity and walk-in closet for master dressing area

design basics inc.
HOME PLAN DESIGN SERVICE

Total Square Footage: 1751

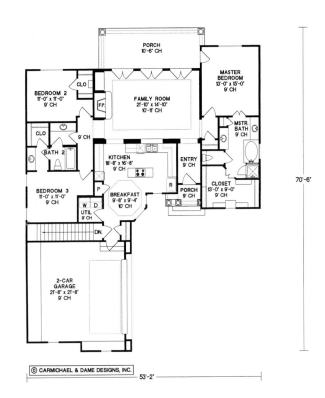

© CARMICHAEL & DAME DESIGNS, INC.

- a charming bayed breakfast area joins a spacious, gourmet kitchen with wrap-around counters, center cook-top and pantry

- gracious family room includes special ceiling detail, a fireplace and three sets of French doors leading to a private porch

- separated from other bedrooms, the luxurious master suite features an over-sized walk-in closet with built-ins, compartmented bath, whirlpool and his and her vanities

- secondary bedrooms enjoy walk-in closets and share a compartmented bath with separate vanities

8068-9G HANCOCK RIDGE
PRICE CODE 17

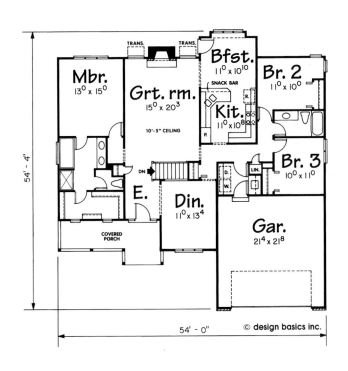

Total Square Footage: 1751

- a friendly covered porch is an ideal spot to watch the play in the front yard

- a half wall in the dining room provides views into the great room while eating

- bedrooms are separated into two wings for privacy within the home itself

4948-9G BRADBURY

PRICE CODE 17

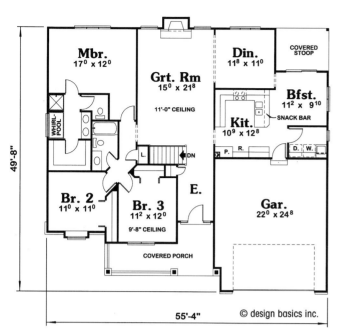

Mbr.
17⁰ x 12⁰

Grt. Rm
15⁰ x 21⁸

11'-0" CEILING

Din.
11⁸ x 11⁰

COVERED STOOP

Bfst.
11² x 9¹⁰

SNACK BAR

Kit.
10⁹ x 12⁸

WHIRL-POOL

49'-8"

Br. 2
11⁰ x 11⁰

Br. 3
11² x 12⁰

9'-8" CEILING

E.

Gar.
22⁰ x 24⁸

P.   R.   D. W.

DN

L.

COVERED PORCH

55'-4"

© design basics inc.

NOTE: 9 FT. MAIN LEVEL WALLS

Total Square Footage: 1758

- the kitchen has a snack bar, breakfast area and pantry, and is near a convenient laundry room off the garage

- the large great room is further volumized by a stairway to the lower level and 11-foot ceiling

- the entry opens dramatically to an impressive volume great room

- the master suite welcomes a shower and whirlpool tub, dual-lavs, compartmental stool and a large walk-in closet

- along with angled entries, bedrooms 2 and 3 enjoy roomy closets and access to a full bath

- a rear covered stoop makes a perfect garden center or sitting stoop

24003-9G TUXFORD

PRICE CODE 17

Total Square Footage: 1762

- from the entry, an archway leads into the breakfast nook, which provides a view to the front

- the large eating bar in the kitchen has room enough for the whole family to enjoy a casual meal

- two additional bedrooms share a full bath and linen closet

- privately located away from the other two bedrooms, the master suite features a corner garden tub with his-and-her vanities to each side

- a row of windows frames a stunning view to the back in the family room with 11-foot ceiling

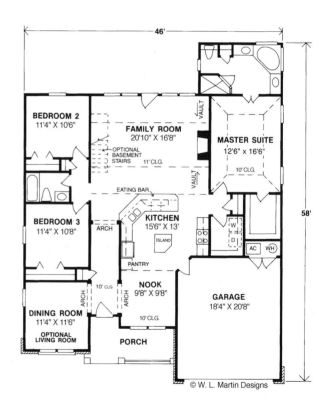

46'

BEDROOM 2
11'4" X 10'6"

FAMILY ROOM
20'10" X 16'8"

OPTIONAL BASEMENT STAIRS

11' CLG.

MASTER SUITE
12'6" X 16'6"

10' CLG.

VAULT

VAULT

EATING BAR

BEDROOM 3
11'4" X 10'8"

ARCH

KITCHEN
15'6" X 13'

ISLAND

58'

W D

AC WH

PANTRY

10' CLG

NOOK
9'8" X 9'8"

ARCH

ARCH

GARAGE
18'4" X 20'8"

DINING ROOM
11'4" X 11'6"

OPTIONAL LIVING ROOM

10' CLG

PORCH

© W. L. Martin Designs

800-947-7526

24026-9G WARREN

PRICE CODE 17

Total Square Footage: 1767

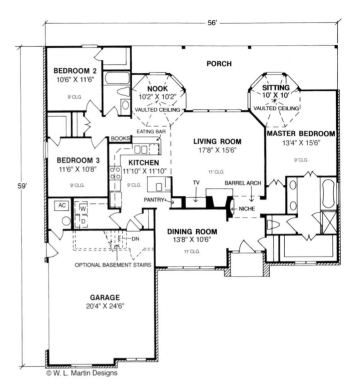

BEDROOM 2
10'6" X 11'6"
9' CLG.

PORCH

NOOK
10'2" X 10'2"
VAULTED CEILING

SITTING
10' X 10'
VAULTED CEILING

EATING BAR

BOOKS

LIVING ROOM
17'8" X 15'6"

MASTER BEDROOM
13'4" X 15'6"
9' CLG.

BEDROOM 3
11'6" X 10'8"
9' CLG.

KITCHEN
11'10" X 11'10"
9' CLG.

11' CLG.

TV

BARREL ARCH

PANTRY

NICHE

AC

W D

DN

DINING ROOM
13'8" X 10'6"
11' CLG.

OPTIONAL BASEMENT STAIRS

GARAGE
20'4" X 24'6"

© W. L. Martin Designs

- the living room has a built-in TV unit beside a fireplace and is visually expanded by the inclusion of a triple rear window and 11-foot ceiling

- a bayed sitting room, as well as a full bath with soaking tub and walk-in closet, highlight the master suite

- a penninsula counter, pantry and eating bar are included in the kitchen

- a pair of rooms with vaulted ceilings located to the rear of the home overlook a large porch, which is perfect for entertaining

5454-9G ANANDALE

PRICE CODE 17

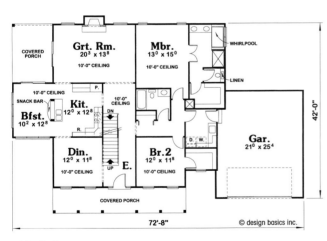

COVERED PORCH

Grt. Rm.
20³ x 13⁸
10'-0" CEILING

Mbr.
13⁰ x 15⁰
10'-0" CEILING

WHIRLPOOL

LINEN

SNACK BAR

10'-0" CEILING

P.

Kit.
12⁰ x 12⁸

10'-0" CEILING

DN

Bfst.
10² x 12⁸

R.

Gar.
21⁰ x 25⁴

Din.
12⁰ x 11⁸
10'-0" CEILING

Br.2
12⁰ x 11⁸
10'-0" CEILING

D. W.

E.

UP

42'-0"

COVERED PORCH

72'-8"

© design basics inc.

NOTE: 9 FT. MAIN LEVEL WALLS

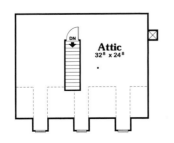

DN

Attic
32⁸ x 24⁸

Total Square Footage: 1768 Optional Finished Attic 841 Sq. Ft.

- a friendly walk-thru kitchen is well-integrated with the dinette and features an island snack bar

- a large attic upstairs lends itself to a hobby room or an extra bedroom suite

- bedroom 2 features a walk-in closet and is across from a full bath

- French doors reveal the master bath with tempting whirlpool tub, dual-lav vanity and convenient walk-in closet

- a front porch lends the feel of times gone by on this Cape Cod-inspired elevation

www.designbasics.com

63

5459-9G LANGSTON

PRICE CODE 17

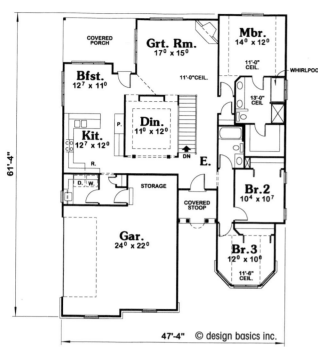

61'-4"

47'-4"   © design basics inc.

NOTE: 9 FT. MAIN LEVEL WALLS

Total Square Footage: 1772

- a central dining room makes an elegant view in the entry and is within steps of the kitchen and great room

- symmetry adds interest to the master bedroom with a vaulted ceiling that centers on an arch-top window

- a rear covered porch creates a secluded getaway spot off the breakfast area

- a workbench easily fits into a storage area in the garage

8067-9G RIVER OAKS

PRICE CODE 17

Total Square Footage: 1775

- a deep front porch offers room for a bench and quiet evening meditation

- a dining room expands into the great room for large gatherings

- two secondary bedrooms with distinct windows provide views to the front

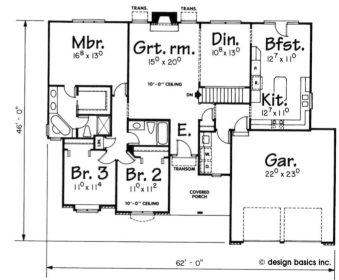

46'-0"

62'-0"   © design basics inc.

CUSTOMIZE
any home plan

design basics inc.
HOME PLAN DESIGN SERVICE

3577-9G BENNETT
PRICE CODE 17

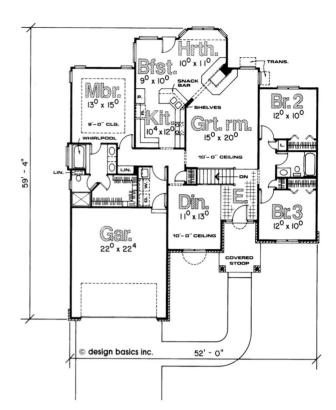

Total Square Footage: 1782

- two secondary bedrooms in separate wing from master suite for added privacy

- arched windows and volume ceiling in dining room capture the eye

- hearth area has bayed windows and shares a three-sided fireplace

- master suite enhanced by large walk-in closet and whirlpool tub

6732-9G WESTFALL
PRICE CODE 18

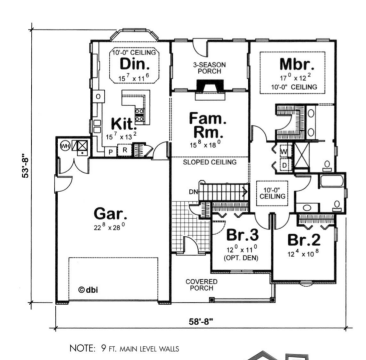

NOTE: 9 FT. MAIN LEVEL WALLS

CUSTOMIZE
any home plan

Total Square Footage: 1784

Call us for more
ADA Designs.

- open spaces, wide hallways and doors and a mechanical room off the garage make this universal home highly accessible

- the combined kitchen and bayed dining room include a center cooktop with snack bar, pantry, hutch and access to a three-season porch

- the luxurious master suite includes spacious walk-in closet and roomy compartmented bath

- a laundry closet is conveniently located near all three bedrooms

www.designbasics.com

5465-9G CHRISTINE

PRICE CODE 17

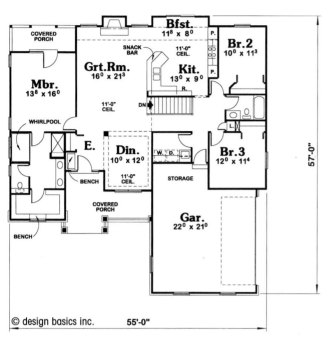

© design basics inc.   55'-0"

57'-0"

NOTE: 9 FT. MAIN LEVEL WALLS

Total Square Footage: 1790

- the central location and integration of the kitchen, great room and breakfast area caters to the modern family's lifestyle

- a large storage area in the garage can be used to place garden and lawn equipment

- built-in benches in the entry and master suite walk-in closet help assist removing shoes getting ready for the day

- a coffered ceiling defines the perimeter of the dining room with beautiful view to the front

6723-9G BOSTWICK

PRICE CODE 17

Total Square Footage: 1791

Call us for more ADA Designs.

- this universal design features three-foot doorways, extra wide hallways and extra open space in closets and baths

- a fireplace and transom-topped, triple-wide window add style to the living room

- the open kitchen and dinette offer a center workspace, roomy hutch, pantries and sliding door leading to a three-season porch

- master bedroom includes small kitchenette, roll-in shower, double vanity and walk-in closet

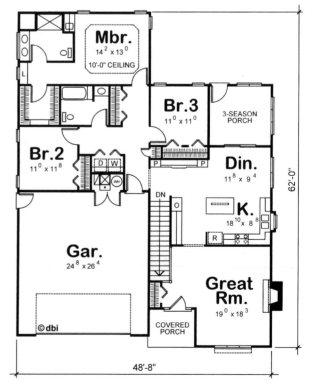

© dbi

48'-8"

62'-0"

NOTE: 9 FT. MAIN LEVEL WALLS

HOME PLAN DESIGN SERVICE

800-947-7526

3298-9G OGDEN

PRICE CODE 17

Total Square Footage: 1793

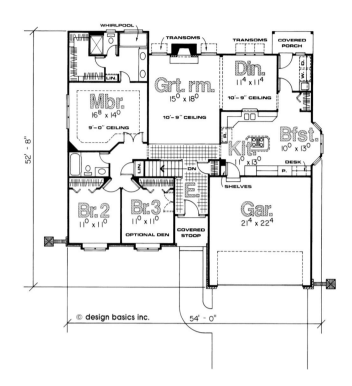

- great room explodes into view with 10'-9" ceiling and lovely windows framing raised hearth fireplace

- volume ceiling and charming windows illuminate formal dining room

- open kitchen includes island cooktop and opening above sink for view of dining room

- bedroom 3 easily converts into den accessed from entry

3587-9G CHARLESTON

PRICE CODE 17

Total Square Footage: 1796

- dining room has 10-foot ceiling and French doors to kitchen/hearth room

- volume ceiling adds spaciousness to great room

- kitchen offers snack bar and views entertainment wall

- screen porch features snack counter

- fireplace and windows brighten hearth room

- dual sink vanity and sunny whirlpool tub capture romance in master bedroom

- bedroom 2 serves as an optional den

8066-9G Hidden Acres

PRICE CODE 18

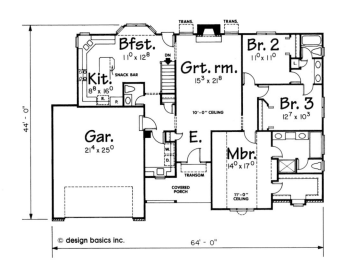

Total Square Footage: 1805

- a generous kitchen provides a snack bar for an informal meal
- large master suite offers a dual-sink vanity, compartmented bath and large walk-in closet
- bayed windows flood the breakfast area with light
- Hollywood bath serves spacious secondary bedrooms

CUSTOMIZE any home plan

5181-9G Vautrin

PRICE CODE 18

Total Square Footage: 1806

- formal meals in the dining room will be easy with a nearby servery
- an angled snack bar in the kitchen offers service to both the breakfast area and great room
- deep window sills create a picturesque atmosphere in the breakfast area
- just off the dinette, a covered porch is a great place to relax in the evening
- a third bedroom is functional as a den and is within steps of a full bath with linen closet
- a volume ceiling adds even more spaciousness to the pampering master suite

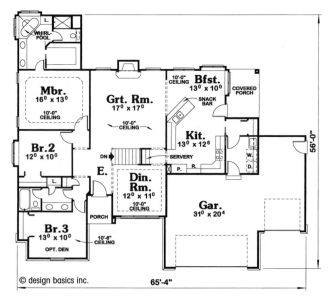

NOTE: 9 FT. MAIN LEVEL WALLS

CUSTOMIZE any home plan

design basics inc.
HOME PLAN DESIGN SERVICE

Total Square Footage: 1806

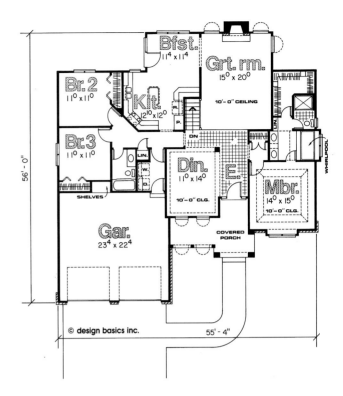

• 10-foot entry has formal views of volume dining room and great room featuring brick fireplace and arched windows

• sunny breakfast room has atrium door to back yard

• garage with built-in shelves accesses home through efficient laundry room

• private master suite includes whirlpool bath with sloped ceiling, plant shelf above dual-lavs and large walk-in closet

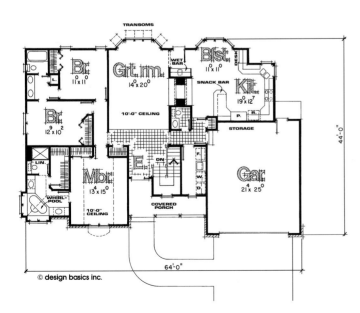

Total Square Footage: 1808

• 10-foot ceilings through entry, great room and staircase

• roomy kitchen with pantry, two lazy Susans and snack bar shares see-thru fireplace with great room

• wet bar/servery between dinette and great room

• master bath has walk-in closet, his-and-her vanities and corner whirlpool tub with windows above

• Hollywood bath for secondary bedrooms

24040-9G HIGHLAND
PRICE CODE 18

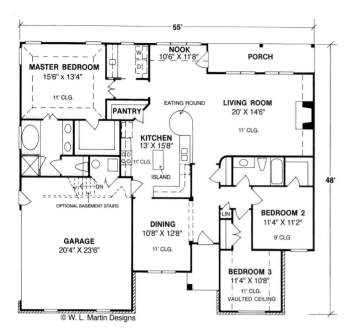

Total Square Footage: 1810

- to the left of the entry, the dining room is just steps from the kitchen

- a walk-in pantry, circular counter and island offer convenience in the kitchen

- the breakfast nook accesses a rear covered porch

- bedroom 3 is made to feel spacious with a volume ceiling, while bedroom 2 offers a walk-in closet

- a combination of brick and siding comprise the elevation of this compact one-story home

8018-9G FOREST GLEN
PRICE CODE 18

Total Square Footage: 1815

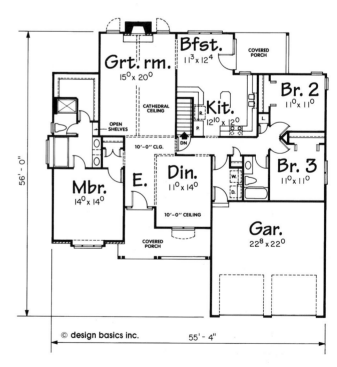

- a cathedral ceiling and transom-topped windows enhance the great room

- a covered porch off the breakfast area offers fresh air and sunshine

- amenities in the master suite include a large closet, open shelves, a dual-sink vanity and sunlit tub

design basics inc.
HOME PLAN DESIGN SERVICE

Total Square Footage: 1819

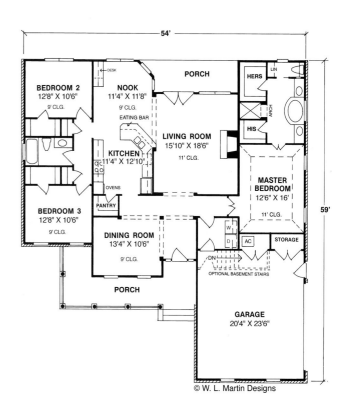

© W. L. Martin Designs

- the kitchen features a walk-in pantry and eating bar that serves the breakfast nook and living room

- french doors lead from the living room onto a rear covered porch

- an 11-foot ceiling towers over the master suite with separate walk-in closets, vanities and a soaking tub

- two additional bedrooms are located on the opposite end of the home from the master suite and feature walk-in closets

- a closet in the garage provides a place for tool storage

3887-9G WINFIELD
PRICE CODE 18

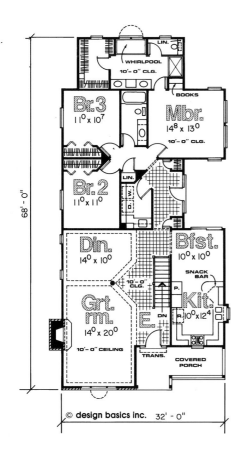

Total Square Footage: 1821

- great room is graced by a palladian arch window and raised-hearth fireplace

- interesting angles and decorative column help define border between great room and formal dining room

- kitchen has generous counter space, pantry, snack bar and plenty of natural light

- deluxe master suite features built-in bookcase, his-and-her vanities, whirlpool tub and walk-in closet

8059-9G INDIAN SPRINGS

PRICE CODE 18

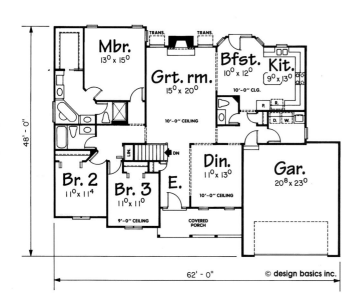

62' - 0"

48' - 0"

Mbr.
13⁰ x 15⁰

Grt. rm.
15⁰ x 20⁰

Bfst.
10⁰ x 12⁰

Kit.
9⁰ x 13⁰

10'-0" CLG.

10'-0" CEILING

Br. 2
11⁰ x 11⁴

Br. 3
11⁰ x 11⁰

E.

Din.
11⁰ x 13⁰

10'-0" CEILING

Gar.
20⁸ x 23⁰

9'-0" CEILING

COVERED PORCH

© design basics inc.

CUSTOMIZE
any home plan

Total Square Footage: 1842

• shutters, double-hung windows and a distinct covered porch coax visitors in

• 10-foot ceilings in all living areas of the home provide a feeling of spaciousness

• master bath offers abundant vanity and dressing space

7214-9G BELWOOD

PRICE CODE 18

Total Square Footage: 1843 Future Expansion 329 Sq. Ft.

• an 11-foot ceiling in the entry and great room give a spacious feel; glass doors flanking the fireplace lead to a screened porch with cathedral ceiling

• a den at the front of the home easily converts to a third bedroom

• amenities in the master suite include special ceiling detail, a charming sitting area, his-and-her vanities, corner whirlpool and walk-in closet

• stairs in the front of the home lead to a finished room over the garage

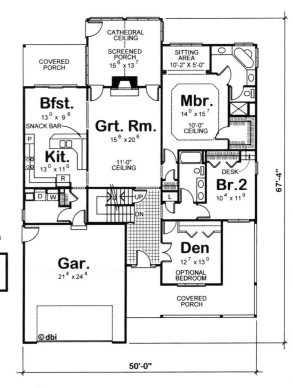

CATHEDRAL CEILING

COVERED PORCH

SCREENED PORCH
15⁶ x 13⁷

SITTING AREA
10'-2" X 5'-0"

Bfst.
13⁰ x 9⁶

SNACK BAR

Kit.
13⁰ x 11⁰

Grt. Rm.
15⁶ x 20⁶

11'-0" CEILING

Mbr.
14⁰ x 15⁷

10'-0" CEILING

DESK

Br. 2
10⁴ x 11⁹

DN

FUTURE EXPANSION
329 SQ. FT.

Gar.
21⁴ x 24⁴

Den
12⁷ x 13⁰

OPTIONAL BEDROOM

COVERED PORCH

© dbi

67'-4"

50'-0"

NOTE: 9 FT. MAIN LEVEL WALLS

design basics inc.
HOME PLAN DESIGN SERVICE

800-947-7526

Total Square Footage: 1849

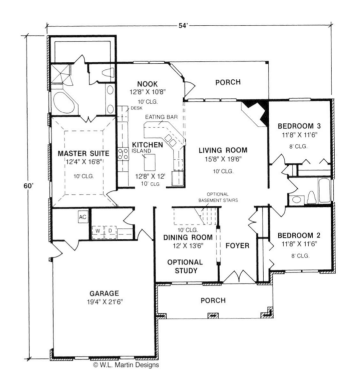

NOOK
12'8" X 10'8"
10' CLG.

DESK

EATING BAR

PORCH

BEDROOM 3
11'8" X 11'6"
8' CLG.

KITCHEN
ISLAND
12'8" X 12'
10' CLG

MASTER SUITE
12'4" X 16'8"
10' CLG.

LIVING ROOM
15'8" X 19'6"
10' CLG.

54'

60'

OPTIONAL
BASEMENT STAIRS

AC

W D

10' CLG.
DINING ROOM
12' X 13'6"

FOYER

BEDROOM 2
11'8" X 11'6"
8' CLG.

OPTIONAL
STUDY

GARAGE
19'4" X 21'6"

PORCH

© W.L. Martin Designs

- a front porch with a pair of brick arches welcomes a bench for relaxing in the outdoors

- easily flexible as a study, the dining room is near the kitchen and features an elegant entry from the foyer

- an abundance of cabinets surround an island counter in the kitchen

- the master suite is separated from two additional bedrooms and features an elegant corner shower, soaking tub and double vanity

- a corner fireplace in the living room is visible from the kitchen and breakfast nook

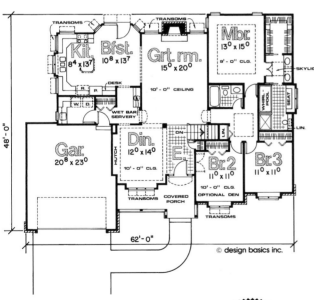

TRANSOMS

TRANSOMS

Kit.
8⁴ x 13⁷

Bfst.
10⁸ x 13⁷

Grt. rm.
15⁰ x 20⁰

Mbr.
13⁰ x 15⁰

9'-0" CLG.

SKYLIGHT

10'-0" CEILING

DESK

WHIRL POOL

SEAT

WET BAR
SERVERY

W. D.

Gar.
20⁸ x 23⁰

Din.
12⁰ x 14⁰

10'-0" CLG.

HUTCH

DN

UP

LIN

Br. 2
11⁰ x 11⁰

10'-0" CLG.
OPTIONAL DEN

Br. 3
11⁰ x 11⁰

48'-0"

COVERED
PORCH

TRANSOMS

TRANSOMS

62'-0"

© design basics inc.

Total Square Footage: 1850

- master suite enjoys decorative boxed ceiling and elegant windows to the rear, dual-lavs, walk-in closet, whirlpool and cedar-lined window seat for storage

- laundry/mud room with sink and extra counter space

- kitchen/dinette area includes bayed eating area, wrapping counters, desk, island and wet bar/servery for entertaining

- bedroom 2 can be utilized as an optional den

www.designbasics.com

8058-9G MORGAN CREEK

PRICE CODE 18

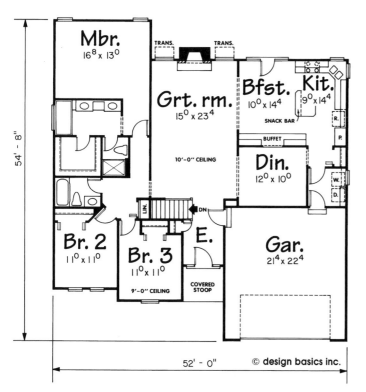

Total Square Footage: 1852

- a generous serving buffet is adjacent to the dining room for serving formal meals

- a snack bar in the kitchen offers a spot for meals on the go

- an extensive great room serves a variety of functions – a path to the bedroom wing, a possible extension of the dining room

- the dining room is a cozy place for an after-dinner cup of coffee

4953-9G MORENCI

PRICE CODE 18

Total Square Footage: 1853

- corner boards and squared columns accent this home

- the large great room is ideally suited to accommodate guests from the entry as well as the dining room

- an angled snack bar in the kitchen makes a great place for an informational meal

- perfect as a in-law suite, bedroom 4 is secluded and offers a 3/4 bath and walk-in closet

NOTE: 9 FT. MAIN LEVEL WALLS

design basics inc.
HOME PLAN DESIGN SERVICE

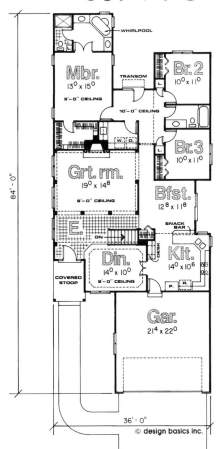

Total Square Footage: 1864

- entry framed by sidelights and detailed trim adds character

- inside, entry views elegant dining room and spacious great room

- French doors access dining room from kitchen which features planning desk, pantry and corner sink with two windows

- laundry, with space for soaking sink, located near bedrooms

© design basics inc.

3299-9G TATUM
PRICE CODE 18

© design basics inc.

Total Square Footage: 1873

- generous 11'-11" ceiling in great room invites guests inside

- French doors add elegance to master bath equipped with leisurely whirlpool tub and double vanity

- secluded bedroom wing

- breakfast area with planning desk connects kitchen and dining room

- back porch is great place to relax

- dining room has views to the back through picturesque windows

www.designbasics.com

9198-9G Windrush Estate
PRICE CODE 18

Total Square Footage: 1876

- a front porch on this sprawling one-story leads inside, where the view passes through the family room and onto the rear porch

- a long island counter seats the whole family for breakfast

- an organized master closet features a window and is steps from the bath with whirlpool tub, double vanity and linen cabinet

---

3891-9G Stockville
PRICE CODE 18

Total Square Footage: 1883

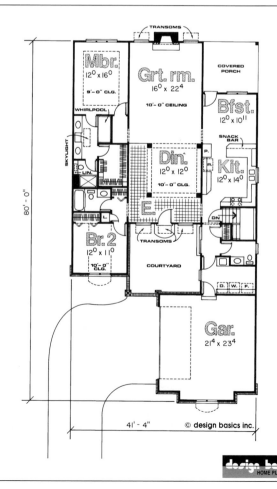

- entrance is granted privacy with spacious front courtyard

- impactful entry offers views through open dining room, to sizeable great room with raised-hearth fireplace

- kitchen adjoins breakfast area with direct access to covered porch

- master suite offers skylit dressing area with double vanity and walk-in closet

3879-9G THOMASVILLE
PRICE CODE 18

Total Square Footage: 1885

- open formal dining room features special ceiling details and a see-thru fireplace

- master bath includes walk-in closet, whirlpool and double vanity under a sloped ceiling

- great room features a flush-hearth fireplace, expansive views to the rear and open access to the dinette

- successive tiers layer the front elevation, providing visual intrigue

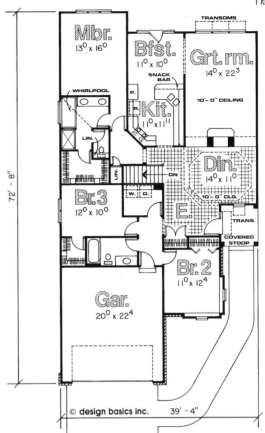

Mbr.
13⁰ x 16⁰

Bfst.
11⁰ x 10⁰

Grt. rm.
14⁰ x 22³

TRANSOMS

WHIRLPOOL

SNACK BAR

10'-0" CEILING

P.

Kit.
11⁰ x 11¹¹

Din.
14⁰ x 11⁰

10'-0" CLG.

LIN.

LIN.

DN

E.

TRANS.

Br. 3
12⁰ x 10⁰

W. D.

COVERED STOOP

Gar.
20⁰ x 22⁴

Br. 2
11⁰ x 12⁴

72' - 8"

© design basics inc.   39' - 4"

5507-9G ELROSE
PRICE CODE 18

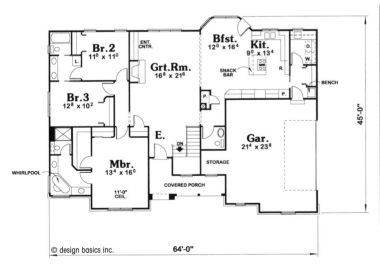

Br. 2
11⁰ x 11⁰

ENT. CNTR.

Bfst.
12⁰ x 16⁴

Kit.
9⁰ x 13⁴

D.

W.

Grt. Rm.
16⁸ x 21⁶

SNACK BAR

R.

BENCH

Br. 3
12⁸ x 10²

P.

P.

E.

DN

Gar.
21⁴ x 23⁸

WHIRLPOOL

Mbr.
13⁴ x 16⁰

STORAGE

COVERED PORCH

11'-0" CEIL.

45'-0"

© design basics inc.   64'-0"

NOTE: 9 FT. MAIN LEVEL WALLS

Total Square Footage: 1886

- a bench near a large closet and laundry room makes it easy to remove muddy apparel when entering from the garage

- Hollywood bath is shared by bedrooms 2 and 3

- home electronic equipment has a place next to the fireplace in the great room

- two pantries and an abundance of cabinet in the kitchen more than accommodate dishes and foodstuffs

www.designbasics.com

2799-9G HAWTHORNE

PRICE CODE 18

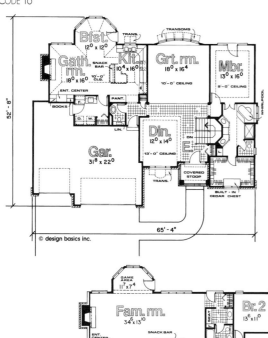

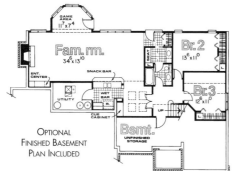

OPTIONAL
FINISHED BASEMENT
PLAN INCLUDED

Total Square Footage: 1887 Optional Finished Basement 1338 Sq. Ft.

- integrated design of gathering room, dinette and kitchen for family living

- master dressing area with angled lavs, make-up counter and walk-in closet

- optional finished basement designed for independent living, with kitchen, bath and private access

CUSTOMIZE
any home plan

5135-9G HAYDEN

PRICE CODE 18

Total Square Footage: 1894

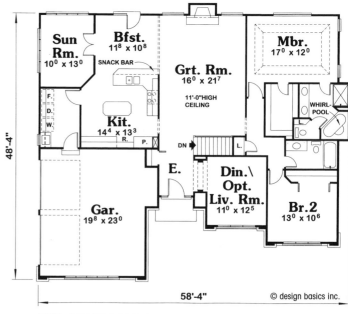

NOTE: 9 FT. MAIN LEVEL WALLS

- sturdy columns framing the wall corners give geometric balance to this home

- traffic flow is enhanced through two entrances into the kitchen which includes an island counter and snack bar

- a tiered entrance brings an old-world feel to the dining room which is optional as a living space

- a large laundry room accommodates a soaking sink and freezer space

design basics inc.
HOME PLAN DESIGN SERVICE

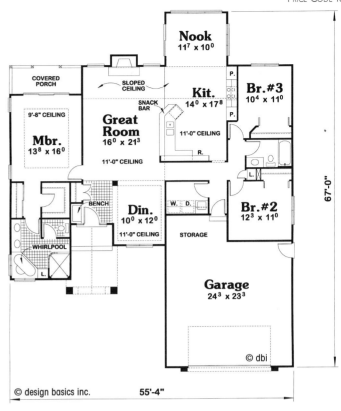

Nook 11⁷ x 10⁰

COVERED PORCH

SLOPED CEILING

9'-8" CEILING

Kit. 14⁰ x 17⁸

SNACK BAR

Br. #3 10⁴ x 11⁰

Great Room 16⁰ x 21³

11'-0" CEILING

Mbr. 13⁸ x 16⁰

11'-0" CEILING

BENCH

Din. 10⁰ x 12⁰

11'-0" CEILING

W. D.

STORAGE

Br. #2 12³ x 11⁰

WHIRLPOOL

Garage 24³ x 23³

© dbi

© design basics inc.

55'-4"

67'-0"

NOTE: 9 FT. MAIN LEVEL WALLS

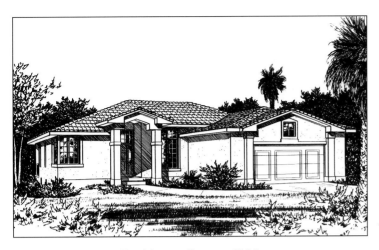

Total Square Footage: 1895

- a simple stucco facade with tile roof and features an entry accented with large columns, sidelites and transom

- the master bedroom leaps out through a nine-foot patio door to a secluded, covered porch

- the master bedroom also offers raised ceiling detail and a master bath

- the great room and kitchen are open to each other and share a sloped ceiling up to 11-feet-high

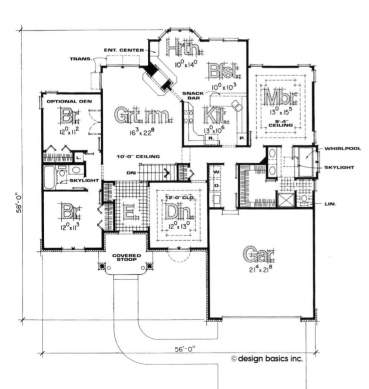

ENT. CENTER
TRANS.
Hrth 10⁰ x 14⁰
Bfst 10⁰ x 10³
SNACK BAR
Mbr 13⁰ x 15⁵
9'-4" CEILING

OPTIONAL DEN
Br 12⁰ x 11²
Gr. rm. 16³ x 22⁸
Kit 13⁰ x 10⁶

WHIRLPOOL
SKYLIGHT

10'-0" CEILING
DN
SKYLIGHT
Br 12⁰ x 11³
Dn. 12⁰ x 13⁰
12'-0" CLG.
W. D.
LIN.

COVERED STOOP
Gar. 21⁴ x 21⁸

58'-0"
56'-0"

© design basics inc.

Total Square Footage: 1911

- beautiful arched dining room window and detailed ceiling to 12-feet-high

- add French doors to bedroom adjacent to great room for optional den, remove closet for built-in bookcase

- see-thru fireplace seen from entry

- master bath area with skylight, whirlpool, his-and-her vanity and walk-in closet

8019-9G HUNTERS CROSSING

PRICE CODE 19

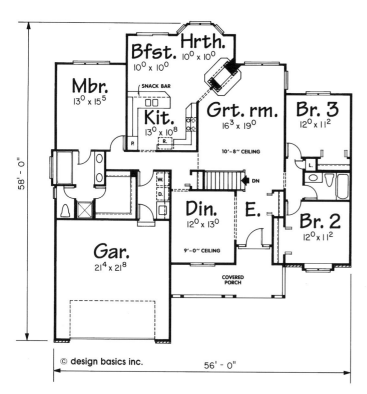

Mbr.
13⁰ x 15⁵

Bfst.
10⁰ x 10⁰

Hrth.
10⁰ x 10⁰

SNACK BAR

Kit.
13⁰ x 10⁸

Grt. rm.
16³ x 19⁰

Br. 3
12⁰ x 11²

10'-8" CEILING

P.

R.

W.
D.

DN

Din.
12⁰ x 13⁰

E.

Br. 2
12⁰ x 11²

9'-0" CEILING

Gar.
21⁴ x 21⁸

COVERED
PORCH

© design basics inc.

56' - 0"

58' - 0"

Total Square Footage: 1919

- wrapping counters and a snack bar in the kitchen make cooking and serving easier

- separate wings for the bedrooms leave options open for office space or serious hobbies

- a angled see-through fireplace provides ambience in the great room and hearth room

5090-9G SIMEON

PRICE CODE 19

Total Square Footage: 1920

- a 10-foot ceiling on the front porch lends a spacious quality

- the living room provides a number of options including use as a third bedroom

- the kitchen and breakfast area create a haven for today's lifestyles

- a walk-in pantry is located near the kitchen, it could also be used for household storage

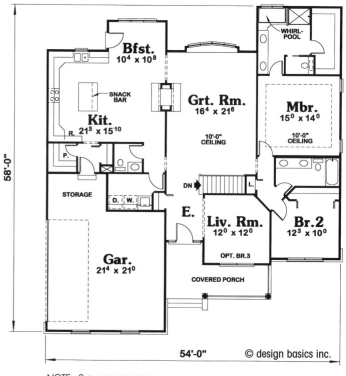

WHIRL-POOL

Bfst.
10⁴ x 10⁸

SNACK BAR

Grt. Rm.
16⁴ x 21⁶

Mbr.
15⁰ x 14⁰

Kit.
21³ x 15¹⁰

10'-0"
CEILING

10'-0"
CEILING

R.

P.

DN

L.

STORAGE

D. W.

E.

Liv. Rm.
12⁰ x 12⁰

Br. 2
12³ x 10⁰

Gar.
21⁴ x 21⁰

OPT. BR.3

COVERED PORCH

58'-0"

54'-0"

© design basics inc.

NOTE: 9 FT. MAIN LEVEL WALLS

design basics inc.
HOME PLAN DESIGN SERVICE

Total Square Footage: 1924

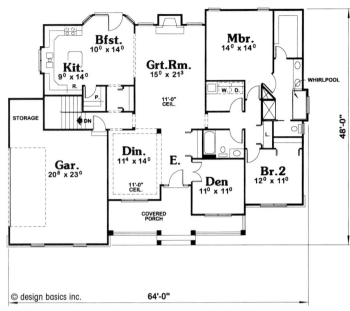

© design basics inc.

64'-0"

48'-0"

NOTE: 9 FT. MAIN LEVEL WALLS

- the home computer can easily be part of the den, located behind a set of double doors

- a front porch bring character to this informal home

- both bedrooms have convenient access to the laundry room, equipped with a soaking sink

- tools and other equipment find a place in an alcove in the garage

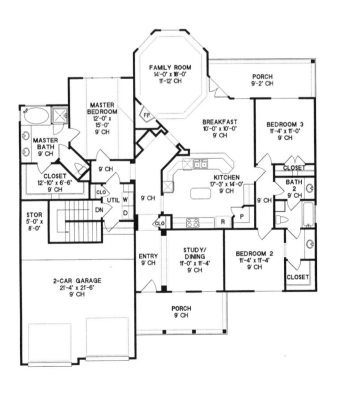

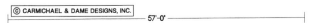

© CARMICHAEL & DAME DESIGNS, INC.

57'-0"

62'-6"

Total Square Footage: 1926

- the subtly arched front porch on this home is elegantly combined with copper accents and a double-gable garage

- an eight-sided family room joins with the rear porch through a set of French doors

- a study easily converts into a dining room and is steps from the kitchen

- counters curve to bring definition to the kitchen, which offers an island and walk-in pantry

www.designbasics.com

5506-9G SPRINGVALE

PRICE CODE 19

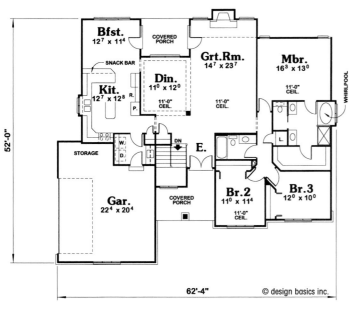

52'-0"

Bfst.
12⁷ x 11⁴

COVERED PORCH

Grt.Rm.
14⁷ x 23⁷

Mbr.
16³ x 13⁰

11'-0" CEIL.

WHIRLPOOL

SNACK BAR

Kit.
12⁷ x 12⁸

Din.
11⁰ x 12⁰

11'-0" CEIL.

11'-0" CEIL.

STORAGE

W. D.

DN

E.

Gar.
22⁴ x 20⁴

COVERED PORCH

Br.2
11⁰ x 11⁴

11'-0" CEIL.

Br.3
12⁰ x 10⁰

62'-4"

© design basics inc.

NOTE: 9 FT. MAIN LEVEL WALLS

Total Square Footage: 1931

- guests are greeted with double doors that open to a wide foyer with options to enter the dining or great rooms

- his-and-her vanities, a round whirlpool tub and a roomy walk-in closet accessorize the master bath

- an island counter creates efficiency in the kitchen and offers additional counter space to prepare meals

- a storage area in the garage makes room for lawn equipment and storage shelves

5515-9G CALDWELL

PRICE CODE 19

Total Square Footage: 1941

- the informal breakfast area access the back and is served by a snack bar

- two sizable linen closets located near the bedrooms, offer welcome space for household storage

- a private covered porch off the master suite makes a great place to unwind

- garage can be converted into a front-load design

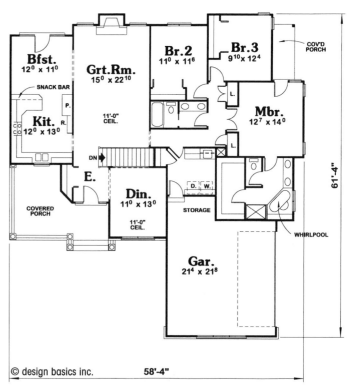

Bfst.
12⁰ x 11⁰

Grt.Rm.
15⁰ x 22¹⁰

Br.2
11⁰ x 11⁶

Br.3
9¹⁰ x 12⁴

COV'D PORCH

SNACK BAR

P.

Kit.
12⁰ x 13⁰

R.

11'-0" CEIL.

Mbr.
12⁷ x 14⁰

DN

E.

COVERED PORCH

Din.
11⁰ x 13⁰

11'-0" CEIL.

D. W.

STORAGE

WHIRLPOOL

Gar.
21⁴ x 21⁸

61'-4"

© design basics inc.

58'-4"

NOTE: 9 FT. MAIN LEVEL WALLS

design basics inc.
HOME PLAN DESIGN SERVICE

Total Square Footage: 1948

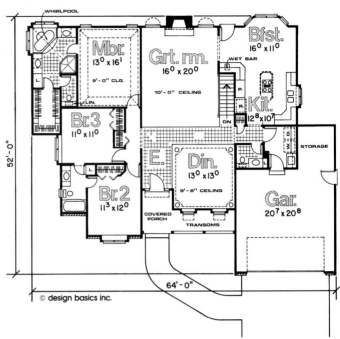

- entry with 10-foot ceiling views open dining room with tapered columns

- pampering master bath with his-and-her vanities, whirlpool, linen cabinet, special shower and walk-in closet

- gourmet kitchen includes island, pantry and wet bar/servery

- great room enjoys a warm fireplace flanked by large windows

3553-9G GLENMORRIE
PRICE CODE 19

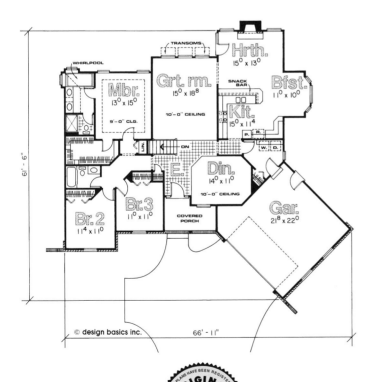

Total Square Footage: 1960

- dining room displays elegance of 10-foot ceiling

- volume great room offers plenty of space and light for gathering

- secluded bedroom wing

- hearth room off the kitchen highlighted with warm fireplace between glass

- master bedroom boasts boxed ceiling

- corner closet in roomy laundry

8046-9G LAUREL GROVE

PRICE CODE 19

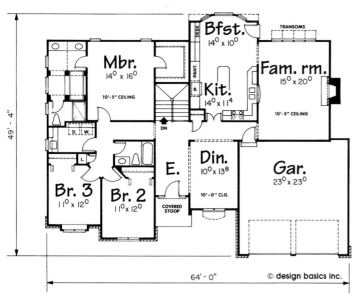

Total Square Footage: 1967

- an elegant dining room offers a pleasant view to the entry
- an island kitchen offers a view into the family room from the sink
- the desk in the breakfast area is a sunny place to balance the checkbook

6803-9G SANTA FE

PRICE CODE 19

Total Square Footage: 1970

- a segmented arch in front of the entrance leads to a covered courtyard with an adjoining open courtyard
- the dining room has three unique windows which provide a lovely view to the courtyard and a tiered ceiling
- an enormous great room shares a see-through fireplace with the hearth room, which opens to the breakfast nook and kitchen

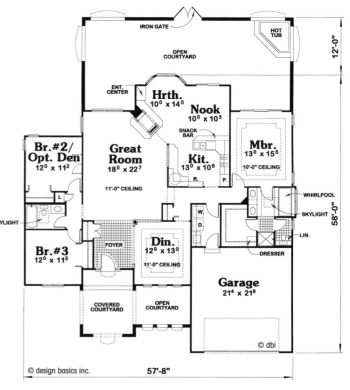

NOTE: 9 FT. MAIN LEVEL WALLS

Total Square Footage: 1971

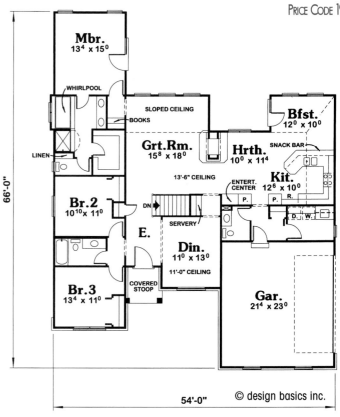

Mbr. 13⁴ x 15⁰

WHIRLPOOL

SLOPED CEILING

BOOKS

LINEN

Grt.Rm. 15⁸ x 18⁰

13'-6" CEILING

Br.2 10¹⁰ x 11⁰

DN

SERVERY

E.

Din. 11⁰ x 13⁰

11'-0" CEILING

COVERED STOOP

Br.3 13⁴ x 11⁰

Bfst. 12⁰ x 10⁰

SNACK BAR

Hrth. 10⁰ x 11⁴

ENTERT. CENTER

Kit. 12⁶ x 10⁰

P.   P.   R.

D. W.

Gar. 21⁴ x 23⁰

66'-0"

54'-0"

© design basics inc.

NOTE: 9 FT. MAIN LEVEL WALLS

- the stately brick exterior of this home beckons interest and attention

- the great room, charmed by a sloped ceiling, shares a see-thru fireplace with the hearth room and kitchen

- the master suite is secluded off the great room and offers private access to outside

- near the kitchen is an efficient laundry room with soaking sink

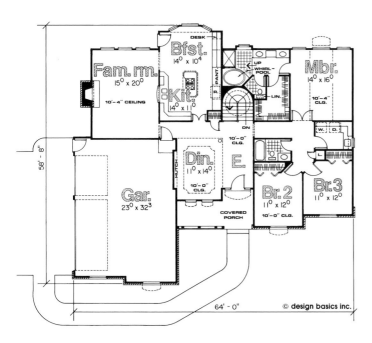

Fam. rm. 15⁰ x 20⁰

10'-4" CEILING

DESK

Bfst. 14⁰ x 10⁴

Kit. 14⁰ x 11⁰

PANT.

UP WHIRL-POOL

LIN.

Mbr. 14⁰ x 16⁰

10'-0" CLG.

DN

10'-0" CLG.

Din. 11⁰ x 14⁰

HUTCH

10'-0" CLG.

E.

W. D.

Br.2 11⁰ x 12⁰

10'-0" CLG.

Br.3 11⁰ x 12⁰

Gar. 23⁰ x 32³

COVERED PORCH

58'-8"

64'-0"

© design basics inc.

CUSTOMIZE
any home plan

Total Square Footage: 1973

- dramatic stairs with dome ceiling above are unique features

- family room has inviting brick fireplace and spacious windows to back

- volume ceiling and arched transom window complement master bedroom

- master bath includes 10' - 4" ceiling, oval whirlpool tub and walk-in closet

- island with cooktop range, roomy pantry and desk highlight kitchen/ dinette area

3031-9G JONESVILLE

PRICE CODE 19

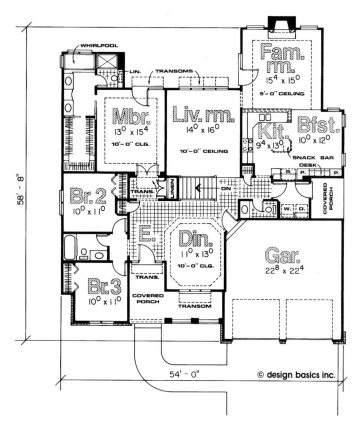

Total Square Footage: 1978

- dramatic formal dining room open to 10-foot-tall entry

- family room open to kitchen and breakfast area provides great atmosphere for informal gatherings

- laundry has access to covered porch

- breakfast area with two pantries and built-in desk complements the island kitchen

- French doors open to master suite, enhanced by private back yard access and whirlpool bath with spacious closet and dual-lavs

24021-9G BARBER

PRICE CODE 19

Total Square Footage: 1980

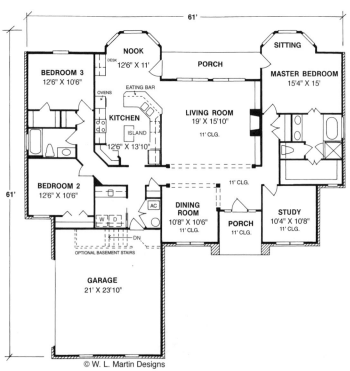

- the foyer, dining and living rooms share the spaciousness of an 11-foot ceiling

- a bayed sitting area provides a place to relax in the master bedroom

- cabinets wrap around a central island for efficiency in the kitchen

- a pair of double windows in the living room overlooks a rear porch

800-947-7526

Total Square Footage: 1996

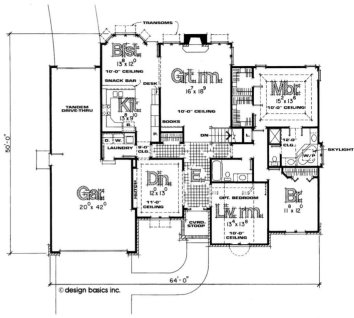

© design basics inc.

- formal dining room with hutch space and tiered ceiling up to 11-feet-high

- combination mud/laundry room for easy access from garage

- skylit master bath with whirlpool, his-and-her vanities and plant ledge

- tandem 3-car drive-through garage

- gorgeous fireplace surrounded by windows in great room with built-in bookcase and 10-foot ceiling

- living room with volume ceiling can become third bedroom

8047-9G MILLERS WAY
PRICE CODE 19

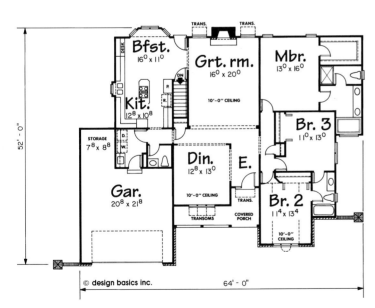

© design basics inc.

Total Square Footage: 1999

- a covered porch may lure one outside during a soft summer rain

- tall windows and ceiling in the dining room add to thoughts of ham and turkey dinners

- a long wall joining the kitchen and breakfast area offers counter space and a desk - places for household planning or homework

2361-9G SUMMERWOOD

PRICE CODE 20

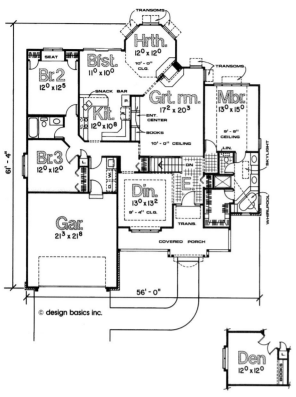

Total Square Footage: 2015

- assets in ideal great room include three-sided see-thru fireplace, entertainment center and bookcases
- kitchen features snack bar, pantry and ample counter space

- window seat framed by closets enhances bedroom 2; bedroom 3 can be converted to an optional den

Den
12⁰ x 12⁰

OPTIONAL DEN

3892-9G TECUMSEH

PRICE CODE 20

Total Square Footage: 2035

- brick wing walls enhance the privacy of this home's romantic front courtyard
- master bedroom with walk-in closet, opens to bath area with corner whirlpool and separate vanities

- entry opens to dramatic views of dining room and great room beyond
- kitchen with snack bar, pantry and plenty of counter space adjoins breakfast area with direct access to covered rear porch

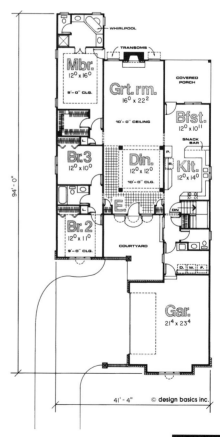

800-947-7526

Total Square Footage: 2039 Unfinished Attic 795 Sq. Ft.

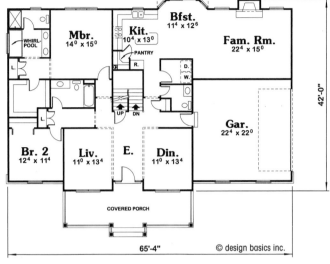

NOTE: 9 FT. MAIN LEVEL WALLS

- oak flooring is abundant throughout the main floor, creating a cozy yet dignified feel

- the master bedroom is located on an opposite wing of the home is furnished with luxurious amenities

- large formal rooms help define the stylish appeal of this design

- an unfinished attic with adorable dormers could be used as a quaint office off guest suite.

5490-9G DENNISON
PRICE CODE 20

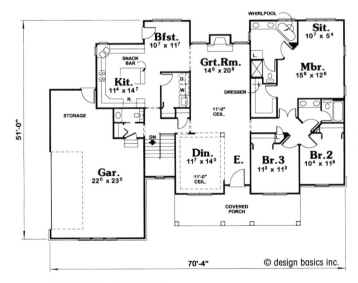

NOTE: 9 FT. MAIN LEVEL WALLS

Total Square Footage: 2040

- an oversized island counter provides abundant workspace in the kitchen

- a sitting room in the master suite offers a place to catch up on reading or office work

- a compartmentalized hall bath allows more than one person to utilize it

- the garage has plenty of storage space for a golf cart

CUSTOMIZE
any home plan

www.designbasics.com

89

9171-9G WESTCOTT MANOR
PRICE CODE 20

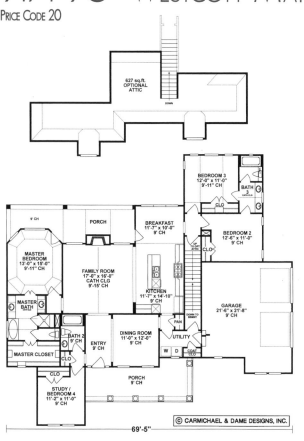

Total Square Footage: 2040 Optional Attic 627 Sq. Ft.

- lap siding and a copper-trimmed roof give refreshing appeal
- second-level attic space makes this home easily expandable
- the master suite is separated from two other bedrooms and is an ideal place to relax on a rear porch or in a bath behind French doors

8122-9G ALBERTA FALLS
PRICE CODE 20

Total Square Footage: 2042

- a covered front porch gives the elevation a warm welcome
- an entry open to the dining room and stairway offers elegant views
- the back of the home boasts a spacious family room, breakfast area and kitchen

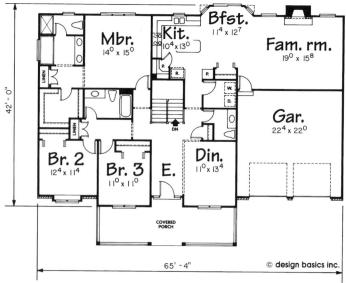

design basics inc.
HOME PLAN DESIGN SERVICE

Total Square Footage: 2047

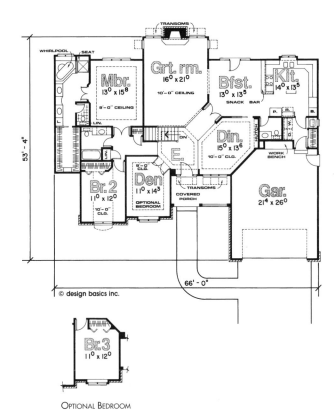

OPTIONAL BEDROOM

- plan allows den off entry to be converted to optional third bedroom

- tall windows, fireplace and 10-foot ceiling adds sophistication to great room

- French doors open to airy dinette/kitchen area with access to outside

- accessed by French doors, the master bedroom features large walk-in closet

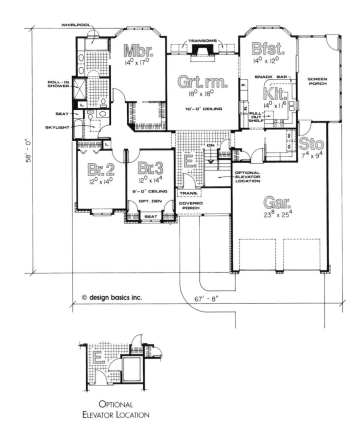

OPTIONAL
ELEVATOR LOCATION

Total Square Footage: 2053

- universally designed home

- sizeable breakfast area shines with bayed windows and access to screen porch

- master suite features bayed window, roomy closet, dressing area, dual-lavs, whirlpool bath and oversized shower

4208-9G CREIGHTON

PRICE CODE 20

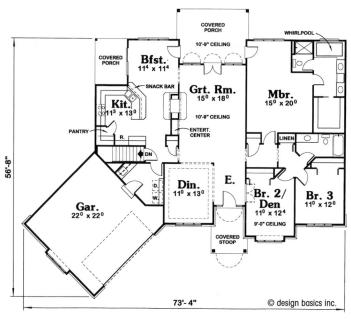

56'-8"

COVERED PORCH
10'-9" CEILING

WHIRLPOOL

COVERED PORCH

Bfst.
11⁴ x 11⁴

SNACK BAR

Grt. Rm.
15⁰ x 18⁰

10'-9" CEILING

Mbr.
15⁰ x 20⁰

Kit.
11³ x 13⁰

PANTRY

R.

ENTERT. CENTER

LINEN

DN

Din.
11⁰ x 13⁰

E.

D.

W.

Gar.
22⁰ x 22⁰

Br. 2/ Den
11⁰ x 12⁴

9'-0" CEILING

Br. 3
11⁰ x 12⁰

COVERED STOOP

73'- 4"

© design basics inc.

NOTE: 8 FT. MAIN LEVEL WALLS

Total Square Footage: 2057

- attractive columns, an angled garage and a stucco veneer dignify this eye-catching home

- the great room featuring a see-through fireplace, entertainment center and French doors to a covered porch

- extra space in the master bedroom provides a place for sitting or work area

- an angled garage makes the home useable on a narrow lot

2222-9G PLAINVIEW

PRICE CODE 20

Total Square Footage: 2068

- elegant covered veranda at entry

- three-sided fireplace serves all gathering areas

- den becomes third bedroom with optional door location

- master suite with private covered deck, dressing area with whirlpool and large walk-in closet

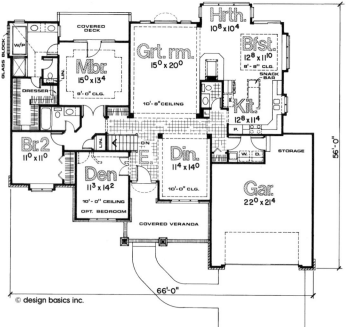

GLASS BLOCK

COVERED DECK

Hrth.
10⁸ x 10⁴

W/P

LIN

Mbr.
15⁰ x 13⁴
8'-0" CLG.

Grt. rm.
15⁰ x 20⁰

10'-8" CEILING

Bfst.
12⁸ x 11¹⁰
8'-8" CLG.

SNACK BAR

DRESSER

Kit.
12⁸ x 11⁴

P.

R.

Br. 2
11⁰ x 11⁰

LIN

DN

STORAGE

W. D.

Den
11³ x 14²
10'-0" CEILING
OPT. BEDROOM

E.

Din.
11⁴ x 14⁰
10'-0" CLG.

Gar.
22⁰ x 21⁴

56'-0"

COVERED VERANDA

© design basics inc.

66'-0"

800-947-7526

Total Square Footage: 2073

© W.L. Martin Designs

- at just 46-feet wide, this home can accommodate a restrictive lot

- a walk-through kitchen features a place for a table and includes a large eating bar

- the family room's fireplace and French-door access to a back porch make it ideal to entertain informally

- the laundry room is conveniently located near three additional bedrooms

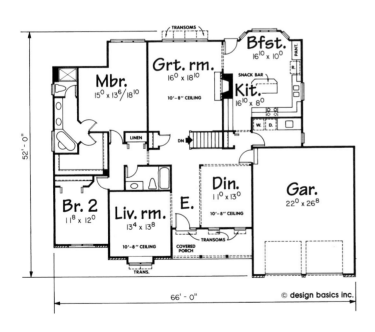

Total Square Footage: 2079

CUSTOMIZE
any home plan

- a fireplace and picture window enhance family activity in the great room

- a well-placed counter in the kitchen makes serving meals in the dining room easier

- large formal rooms provide ample space to entertain

- the master suite has a sitting area with abundant sunlight for relaxing or working

www.designbasics.com

3303-9G RICHARDSON

PRICE CODE 20

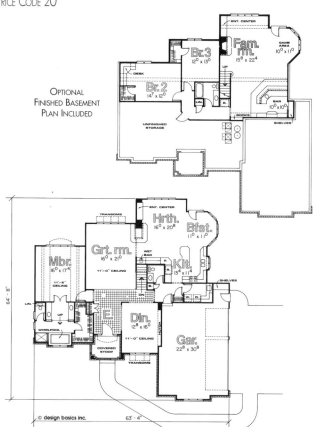

OPTIONAL
FINISHED BASEMENT
PLAN INCLUDED

Total Square Footage: 2083 Optional Finished Basement 1403 Sq. Ft.

- gourmet kitchen features wrapping cabinets, island, double oven and pantry

- hearth room with entertainment center shares three-sided fireplace with great room

- optional finished basement plan shows secondary bedrooms, informal living area and plenty of storage

2454-9G PICKFORD

PRICE CODE 20

Total Square Footage: 2093

- 10-foot ceiling in great room with raised hearth fireplace and windows with arched transoms above

- formal dining room close to great room and kitchen area affords entertaining ease

- island kitchen and bayed dinette with outside access features desk and pantry

- comfortable secondary bedrooms are apart from private master suite

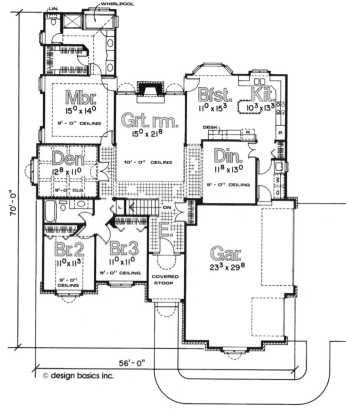

Total Square Footage: 2117

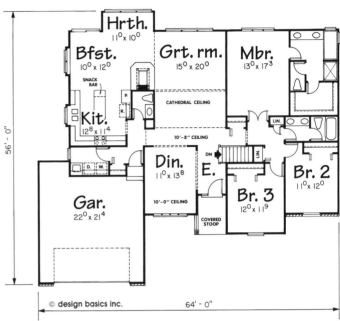

56' - 0"

64' - 0"

© design basics inc.

- a 10-foot dining room ceiling adds elegance to a formal meal

- windows all along the great room, hearth room and breakfast area offer outdoor views

- a three-sided fireplace projects warmth to these areas - whether eating or just relaxing

3196-9G GALLOWAY
PRICE CODE 21

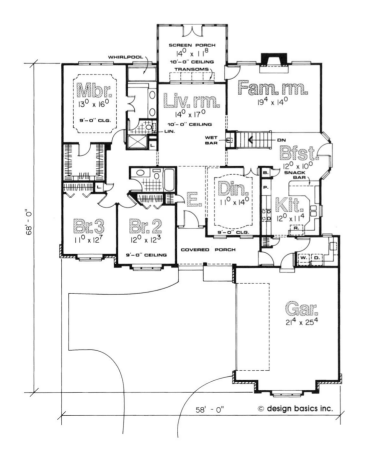

68' - 0"

58' - 0"   © design basics inc.

Total Square Footage: 2120

- ceiling details enhance formal dining room

- breakfast/kitchen area boasts broom closet, snack bar, pantry and lazy Susans

- formal living room has view of screen porch through spacious windows

- family room is warmed by fireplace and provides access to screen porch

24038-9G Clarkson
PRICE CODE 21

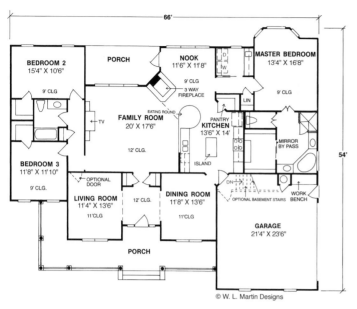

© W. L. Martin Designs

Total Square Footage: 2126

- a 12-foot ceiling in the entry steps down to 11-feet in the adjacent living and dining rooms

- a built-in entertainment center in the family room offers a place for home electronics

- a three-sided fireplace brings warmth to the kitchen, breakfast nook and family room

- front and rear porches are great places to enjoy leisure time

3597-9G Concorde
PRICE CODE 21

Total Square Footage: 2132

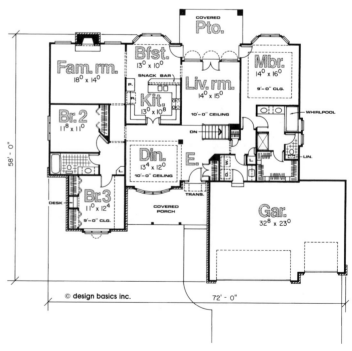

© design basics inc.

- oak entry views elegant living room with French doors to covered patio

- raised hearth fireplace warms secluded family room

- sunny whirlpool and walk-in closet complete master suite

- secondary bedrooms in secluded wing afford privacy for master suite

design basics inc.
HOME PLAN DESIGN SERVICE

Total Square Footage: 2133

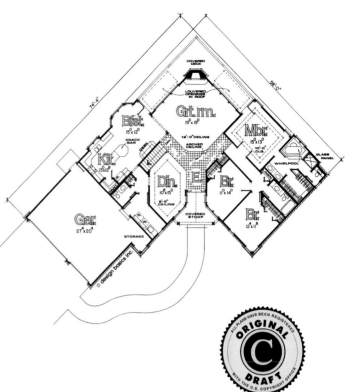

- entry views volume great room with fireplace flanked by windows

- island kitchen with snack bar, desk and walk-in pantry

- romantic master bath with whirlpool, double vanity and walk-in closet

- three-car garage with extra storage space accesses home through mud/laundry room

- double doors lead to master bedroom with tiered ceiling and access to covered deck

3145-9G GREGORY
PRICE CODE 21

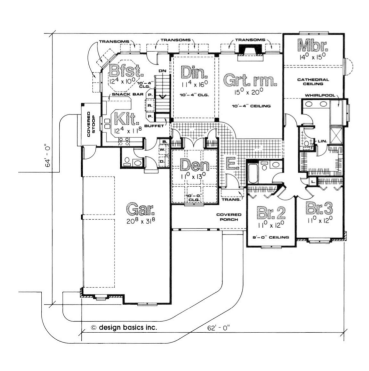

Total Square Footage: 2141

- formal entry views great room and dining room with 10'-4" ceilings

- angled breakfast area with octagon ceiling detail is accessible to kitchen and dining room

- peninsula kitchen features snack bar, two pantries and buffet

- separated dressing area, whirlpool bath and walk-in closet complement this master suite

5508-9G KAROLINE

Price Code 21

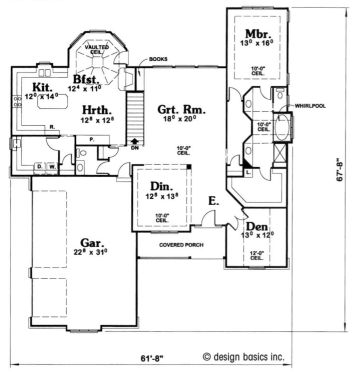

61'-8"

© design basics inc.

NOTE: 9 FT. MAIN LEVEL WALLS

Total Square Footage: 2143

- the dining and great rooms make a natural combination when entertaining guests
- home office workers will enjoy the privately-located den with 12-foot ceiling
- the breakfast area is defined by bayed windows and a vaulted ceiling
- in the master suite, separate vanities and luxurious whirlpool tub create spacious dressing areas

24027-9G OAKLAND

Price Code 21

Total Square Footage: 2144

- a gable extension and columns form a wide stoop on this home's front porch
- three additional bedrooms are separated from the master suite and share a bath divided into compartments
- symmetrical arches grant views into the study and dining room
- a walk-in pantry and island with eating bar serve the kitchen

© W. L. Martin Designs

CUSTOMIZE
any home plan

design basics inc.
HOME PLAN DESIGN SERVICE

Total Square Footage: 2144

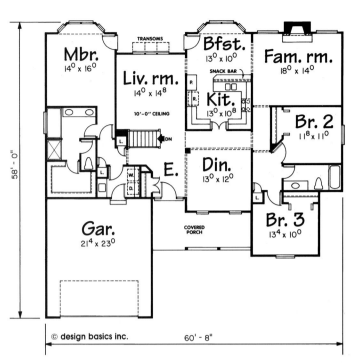

• a family room is secluded for day-to-day living, and a living room is open for easy entertaining

• the kitchen, with wrapping counters, is perfectly situated to serve the dining room and breakfast area

• separate bedroom wings offer privacy and options to convert bedrooms into living space

2848-9G ROXBURY
PRICE CODE 21

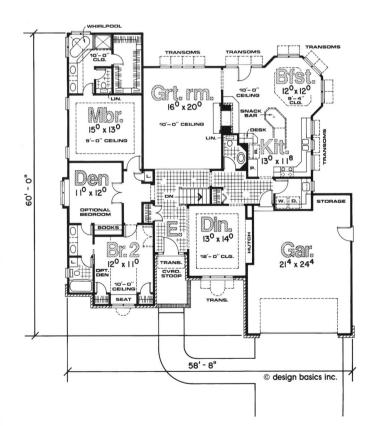

Total Square Footage: 2148

• long views through great room create sense of spaciousness

• formal dining room with hutch space and 12-foot-high ceiling

• island kitchen includes 42" pantry, planning desk and snack bar

• private master suite bath area with plant shelf and step-up whirlpool

2213-9G ESSEX

PRICE CODE 21

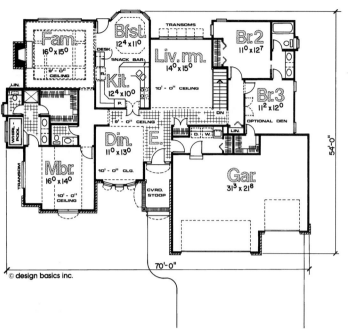

Total Square Footage: 2149

- service doors to close off kitchen from entry and dining room

- open staircase for future finished basement

- private master suite with walk-in closet, double vanity and whirlpool under windows

- open entry views formal rooms

8045-9G COOPERS FARM

PRICE CODE 21

Total Square Footage: 2151

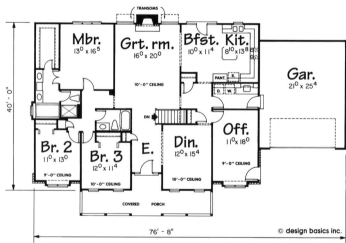

- breezy front porch is a great place to sit and catch up with the day

- a lovely window in the master suite, provides a view of the back as well as a good light source for reading

- office space offers a separate outdoor entrance for clients

- the kitchen, breakfast area and great room, freely open to one another

800-947-7526

Total Square Footage: 2167

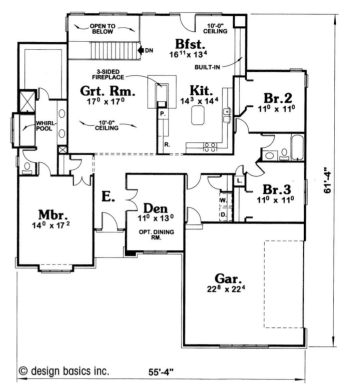

Bfst.
16¹¹ x 13⁴

OPEN TO BELOW

DN

10'-0" CEILING

BUILT-IN

3-SIDED FIREPLACE

Grt. Rm.
17⁰ x 17⁰

Kit.
14³ x 14⁴

Br.2
11⁰ x 11⁰

10'-0" CEILING

WHIRL-POOL

P.

R.

Mbr.
14⁰ x 17²

E.

Den
11⁰ x 13⁰

OPT. DINING RM.

Br.3
11⁰ x 11⁰

W.
D.

L.

Gar.
22⁸ x 22⁴

61'-4"

© design basics inc.

55'-4"

NOTE: 9 FT. MAIN LEVEL WALLS

- a prairie influence brings refreshing symmetry to the front elevation

- separated for privacy, two secondary bedrooms share a full bath

- a stairway in the great room leads to the lower level and is open to two-story-high windows with a view to the back

CUSTOMIZE
any home plan

Total Square Footage: 2172

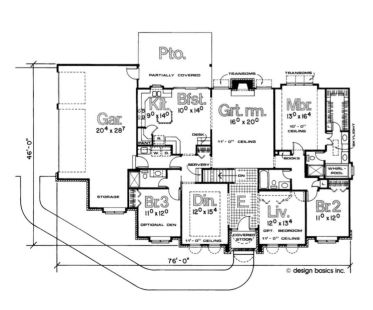

Pto.

PARTIALLY COVERED

TRANSOMS

TRANSOMS

Gar.
20⁴ x 28⁷

Kit.
9⁰ x 14⁰

Bfst.
10⁰ x 14⁰

Grt. rm.
16⁰ x 20⁰

Mbr.
13⁰ x 16⁴

10'-0" CEILING

DESK

11'-0" CEILING

SKYLIGHT

SERVERY

BOOKS

PANTRY

W. D.

DN

WHIRL-POOL

L.

46'-0"

STORAGE

Br.3
11⁰ x 12⁰

OPTIONAL DEN

Din.
12⁰ x 15⁴

11'-0" CEILING

E.

COVERED STOOP

Liv.
12⁰ x 13⁴

OPT. BEDROOM

11'-0" CEILING

Br.2
11⁰ x 12⁰

76'-0"

© design basics inc.

- formal living and dining rooms flanking entry give ease in entertaining

- impressive great room with 11-foot ceiling and picture/awning windows framing a raised-hearth fireplace

- attractive kitchen/dinette area with island, desk, wrapping counters, walk-in pantry and access to covered patio

3005-9G WRENWOOD

PRICE CODE 21

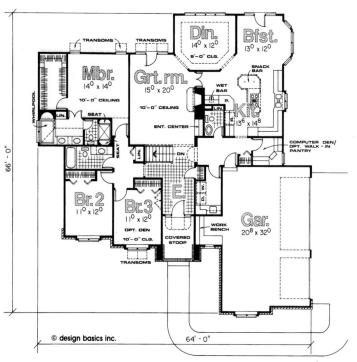

Total Square Footage: 2186

- bright 12-foot-tall entry views large great room with entertainment center, brick fireplace and direct access to dining room and kitchen

- master suite has spacious walk-in closet, lavish whirlpool bath and 10-foot ceiling in bedroom

- bedroom 3 offers versatile den option

- utility corridor has laundry room to one side and computer center to the other

- three-car garage has sunlit shop area

3598-9G BRENTWOOD

PRICE CODE 21

Total Square Footage: 2187

- multiple arched windows accentuate impressive great room

- French doors reveal master suite with walk-in closet, oval whirlpool and double sink vanity

- snack bar and island counter equip kitchen and breakfast area

- bedroom 2 easily converts to a den

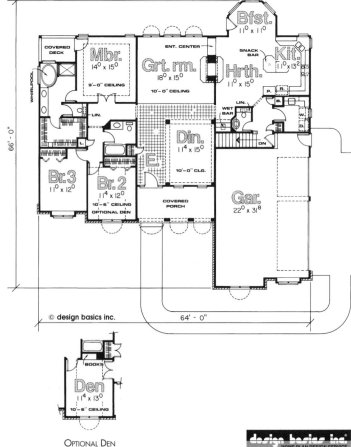

OPTIONAL DEN

© design basics inc.

Total Square Footage: 2188

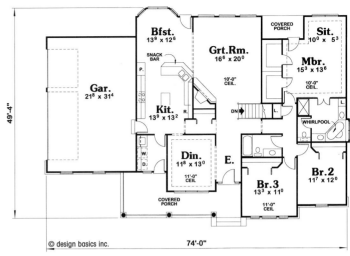

NOTE: 9 FT. MAIN LEVEL WALLS

- the kitchen offers the advantage of a snack bar that serves both the breakfast area and great room

- a three-car garage provides added room for storage of a third vehicle

- the master suite offers a private sitting area, covered porch, his-and-her walk-in closets, separate vanities and corner whirlpool tub

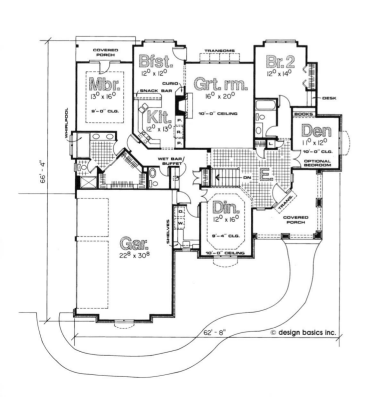

Total Square Footage: 2199

- grand entry hall has views to formal dining room, great room and den with bedroom option

- volume great room has fireplace and cased opening to breakfast area with back yard access

- curio cabinet and two pantries highlight peninsula kitchen

- master suite offers private covered porch and whirlpool bath

9206-9G WINSTON COURT

PRICE CODE 22

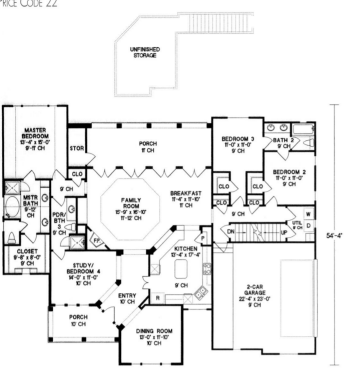

© CARMICHAEL & DAME DESIGNS, INC.

68'-0"

Total Square Footage: 2203

- arches frame the entry into the study, which catches views of a rear porch and breakfast room

- by opening four sets of French doors, the porch becomes an integrated part of the main living areas

- the beauty of this home's stone and siding exterior hides its functional interior layout that offers a variety of shared vistas

6268-9G KNOLLWOOD

PRICE CODE 22

Total Square Footage: 2205

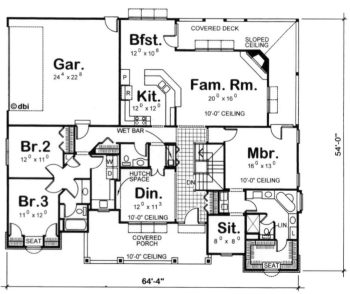

NOTE: 9 FT. MAIN LEVEL WALLS

- 10-foot ceilings throughout living areas and master bedroom add a sense of spaciousness

- dining room features transom-topped windows with view of porch, special hutch space and nearby wet bar

- master suite enjoys wet bar, private sitting area, his-and-her vanities, corner whirlpool and walk-in closet with window seat

- corner fireplace and transom-topped windows enhance the family room

9185-9G LONGWORTH ESTATE
PRICE CODE 22

Total Square Footage: 2211

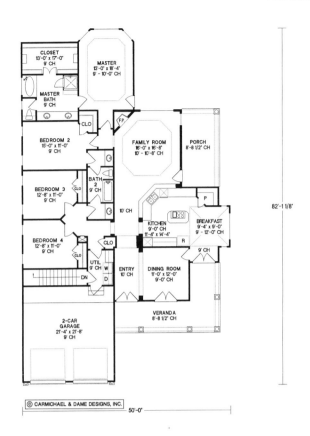

- three sets of double doors attach themselves to the front, wrap-around veranda

- the kitchen features a walk-in pantry, island counter and snack bar

- a bath with split vanities serves three bedrooms in a segregated wing that includes the master suite in a rear corner

© CARMICHAEL & DAME DESIGNS, INC.

4998-9G HOLDEN
PRICE CODE 22

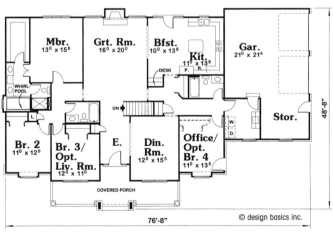

NOTE: 9 FT. MAIN LEVEL WALLS

CUSTOMIZE
any home plan

Total Square Footage: 2227

- a dining room and great room both offer ample space for entertaining

- secluded down a hall, is a private office providing the option of becoming a fourth bedroom

- the kitchen and breakfast area open spaciously to the great room, and have a convenient island, planning desk and pantry

2934-9G OSAGE

PRICE CODE 22

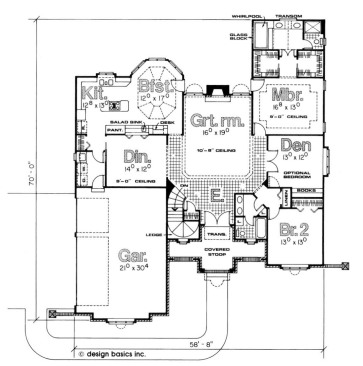

Total Square Footage: 2233

- symmetry, brick details and simple roof lines combine to produce an elegant elevation

- gourmet kitchen features double oven, large pantry and pass-thru buffet

- beautifully vaulted ceiling in breakfast area enhances informal meals

- bedroom 2 and optional bedroom 3/den share compartmented bath

8121-9G NELSONS LANDING

PRICE CODE 22

Total Square Footage: 2241

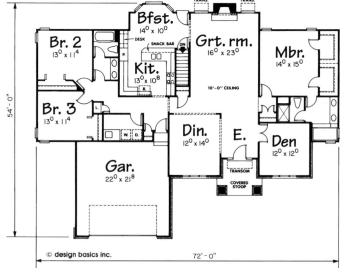

- French doors seclude the den in peace and quiet

- a bayed breakfast area has access to the back for some fresh air after a meal

- the master bedroom offers a compartmented dressing area that doesn't compromise the need for space

CUSTOMIZE
any home plan

design basics inc.
HOME PLAN DESIGN SERVICE

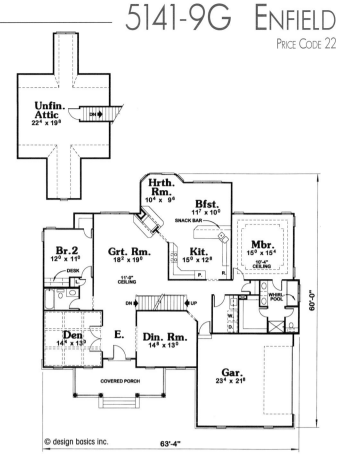

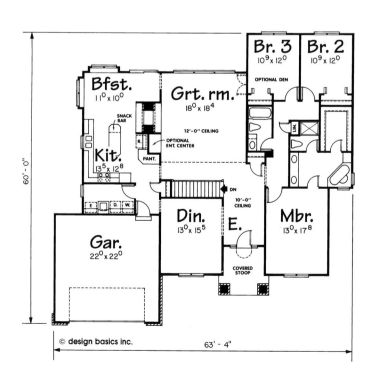

Total Square Footage: 2242 Unfinished Attic 613 Sq. Ft.

- the serene nature of this front elevation will complement almost any neighborhood

- an attic with two long dormers adds ambiance and romance to this home

- the see-thru fireplace warms both the great room and hearth room

- both the dining room and the garage have stream-lined access to the kitchen

© design basics inc.

NOTE: 9 FT. MAIN LEVEL WALLS

Total Square Footage: 2246

- this home has a wide, columned, unforgettable stoop

- a tall entry and even taller great room offer spacious day-to-day living

- a see-thru fireplace provides ambience in the kitchen and eating in the breakfast area

© design basics inc.

24002-9G HANSON

PRICE CODE 22

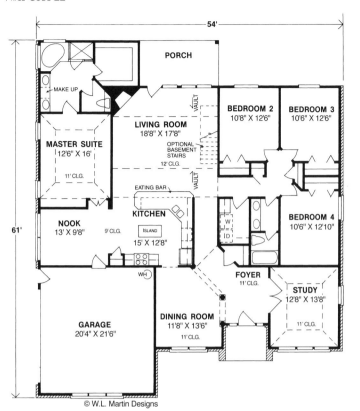

PORCH

MAKE UP

MASTER SUITE
12'6" X 16'
11' CLG.

LIVING ROOM
18'8" X 17'8"
OPTIONAL
BASEMENT
STAIRS
12' CLG.

VAULT

BEDROOM 2
10'8" X 12'6"

BEDROOM 3
10'6" X 12'6"

61'

NOOK
13' X 9'8"
9' CLG.

EATING BAR

KITCHEN
ISLAND
15' X 12'8"

VAULT

W
D

BEDROOM 4
10'6" X 12'10"

WH

GARAGE
20'4" X 21'6"

DINING ROOM
11'8" X 13'6"
11' CLG.

FOYER
11' CLG.

STUDY
12'8" X 13'8"
11' CLG.

54'

© W.L. Martin Designs

Total Square Footage: 2250

- this home's all brick facade showcases elegant windows in the garage, dining room and study

- the study is located behind double doors and features an 11-foot ceiling

- meals can be enjoyed at the eating bar of the kitchen or in the sun-filled breakfast nook

- a rear, covered porch extends the enjoyment of the living room

1388-9G BEAUMONT

PRICE CODE 22

Total Square Footage: 2254

- floor-to-ceiling windows in great room seen from entry

- master bath includes double vanity, step-up whirlpool, large walk-in closet and glass block wall at shower

- see-thru fireplace centered under cathedral ceiling in great room

- optional den or bedroom with French doors

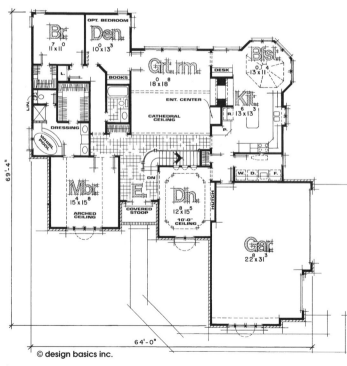

Br.
11⁰x11⁰

Den.
10⁰x13³

OPT. BEDROOM

Grt. rm.
18⁰x18

Bfst.
13¹x14

Kit.
13x13

ENT. CENTER

CATHEDRAL CEILING

DESK

BOOKS

DRESSING

WHIRL POOL

69'-4"

Mbr.
15⁴x15⁸
ARCHED CEILING

DN

COVERED STOOP

Dn.
12⁸x15⁴
10'-0" CEILING

HUTCH

W D F

Gar.
22⁸x31³

64'-0"

© design basics inc.

9189-9G ALEXANDER COURT
PRICE CODE 22

Total Square Footage: 2256

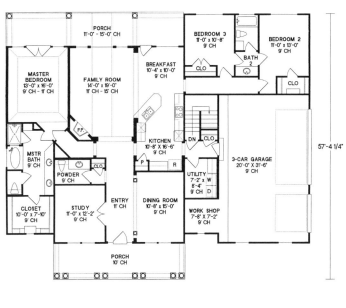

© CARMICHAEL & DAME DESIGNS, INC.

67'-8"

- the rear porch on this home is divided into three visual segments

- a sloped ceiling in the family room extends onto the central portion of the porch

- French doors in the master suite open onto another segment

- the porch off the breakfast area provides a place to enjoy a meal in the fresh air

5516-9G WILDWOOD
PRICE CODE 22

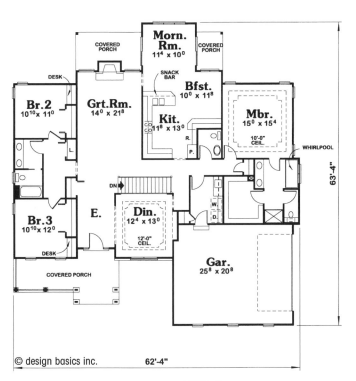

© design basics inc.   62'-4"

NOTE: 9 FT. MAIN LEVEL WALLS

Total Square Footage: 2266

- visible upon entry, an intricately detailed dining room harkens the romance of this design

- a ceiling tiers to 10-feet in height in the privately-located master suite

- two rear porches are great places to enjoy the outdoors

- a hanging closet and soaking sink offer functionality to the laundry room

3523-9G BLANCHARD

Price Code 22

Total Square Footage: 2274

- entry presents bowed dining room

- volume 11'-foot ceiling gives elegance to living room

- walk-in pantry and angled island counter in kitchen

- octagonal breakfast area surrounded with gorgeous views

- master suite has two pairs of French doors; one leading to a large walk-in closet and the other revealing a romantic bayed whirlpool tub

2321-9G ABERDEEN

Price Code 22

Total Square Footage: 2276

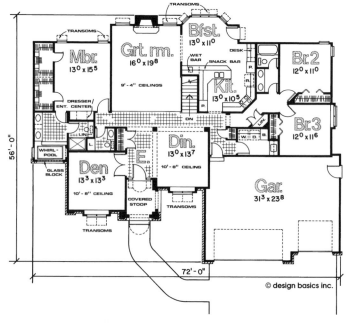

- expansive entry views den with French doors and open dining room

- gourmet kitchen and bayed breakfast area features wet bar/servery, wrapping counters and desk

- secluded secondary bedrooms enhanced by easy access to compartmented bath with two lavs

- master suite has his/her closets and built-in dresser/entertainment center

800-947-7526

design basics inc.
HOME PLAN DESIGN SERVICE

Total Square Footage: 2293

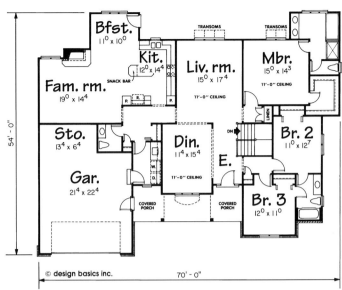

© design basics inc.

- the formal living and dining rooms enjoy 11-foot ceilings and long, pleasing views

- a corner fireplace serves the open family room, breakfast area and kitchen

- a sunny breakfast area leads to the backyard

- a volume ceiling, walk-in closet and compartmented bath enhance the master suite

24030-9G ROYSTON
PRICE CODE 22

© W. L. Martin Designs

Total Square Footage: 2297

- the study is perfect for time alone with its double doors and 11-foot ceiling

- the kitchen is open to the living room and serves the breakfast area with eating bar

- separated from the master suite, three additional bedrooms offer walk-in closets

- a game room provides a second living space for children and guests

8048-9G SYDNEY LANE
PRICE CODE 22

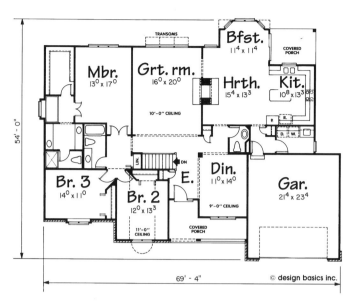

Total Square Footage: 2298

- front and back porches offer the best of the outdoors
- great room shares see-thru fireplace with the hearth room
- two sets of French doors adorn the master suite

7215-9G WHEATLAND
PRICE CODE 22

Total Square Footage: 2299 Future Expansion 338 Sq. Ft.

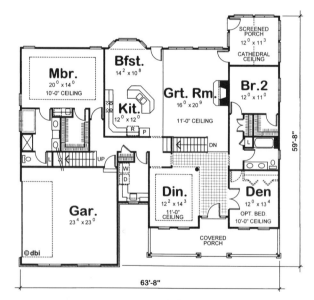

NOTE: 9 FT. MAIN LEVEL WALLS

FUTURE EXPANSION

- open living spaces in the back of the home and an 11-foot ceiling in the great room create a sense of spaciousness
- a bonus room over the garage provides room for future expansion
- a screened porch with cathedral ceiling is accessed from the great room
- master suite enjoys wet bar, 10-foot, boxed ceiling, whirlpool and walk-in closet

3058-9G MONTGOMERY

PRICE CODE 23

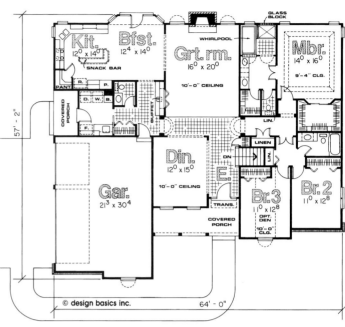

Total Square Footage: 2311

- great room highlighted by pass thru wet bar/buffet

- kitchen features walk-in pantry and wrapping island snack bar

- ample laundry room has desirable access to covered service porch

- corridor design offers privacy between master suite and secondary bedrooms

2651-9G FAIRWAY

PRICE CODE 23

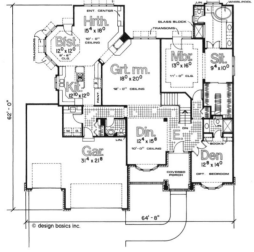

OPTIONAL FINISHED BASEMENT PLAN INCLUDED

Total Square Footage: 2317 Optional Finished Basement 1475 Sq. Ft.

- three-sided fireplace joins great and hearth rooms together in perfect harmony

- charming sitting room and spacious walk-in closet in master bedroom

- optional finished lower level plan (included) features see-thru fireplace, kitchenette and entertainment center

9207-9G Briar Manor

Price Code 23

Total Square Footage: 2331

- grand entrance leads to a combination dining/living room with fireplace and view of the back porch

- bayed master bedroom connects to luxurious master bath with corner whirlpool, dual-lavs and large walk-in closet

- a general pantry and extensive wrapping cabinets provide ample storage in the kitchen

- special ceiling detail creates an octagon-shaped family room with fireplace on one end and access to the porch on the other

24033-9G Malone

Price Code 23

Total Square Footage: 2334

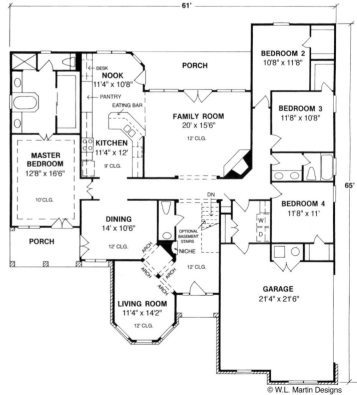

- a corner fireplace, 12-foot ceiling and French doors that open onto a rear porch complete the family room

- three additional bedrooms are separated form the master suite and have walk-in closets

- the foyer includes a built-in niche and has a view of the living room and dining room through a series of arched openings

800-947-7526

Total Square Footage: 2335

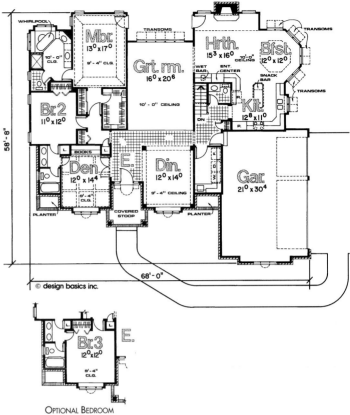

- 10-foot-high entry surveys den, dining room and great room

- lovely den with double doors, spider-beam ceiling, bookcases and bathroom access could easily convert to a bedroom

- spacious hearth room with window-flanked fireplace, wet bar, entertainment center and door to outside

- master bedroom features vaulted ceiling, his-and-her closets and door to outside

OPTIONAL BEDROOM

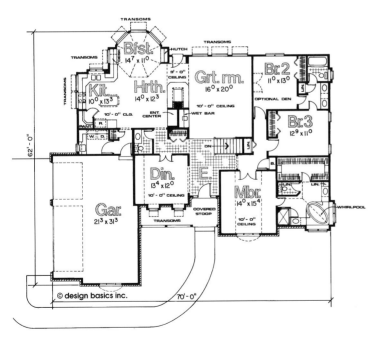

CUSTOMIZE
any home plan

Total Square Footage: 2355

- spectacular three-sided fireplace for great room and hearth room

- luxurious master dressing area with his-and-her vanities, angled oval whirlpool and large walk-in closet

- formal ceiling and boxed windows accent dining room

- open kitchen with island counter and walk-in corner pantry

www.designbasics.com

115

3524-9G TANGENT

PRICE CODE 23

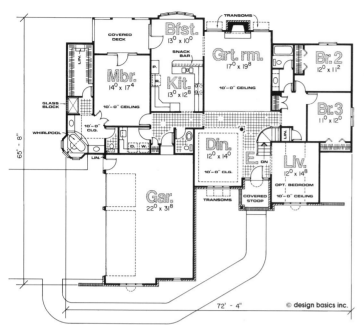

Total Square Footage: 2366

- living room offers 10'-foot ceiling and opts as fourth bedroom

- bowed windows in breakfast area and snack bar peninsula in kitchen

- combined great room, kitchen and breakfast area convenient for family

- 10'-foot ceiling in master bedroom with access to private deck

- master bath highlights include corner whirlpool tub, his-and-her vanities and large walk-in closet

7213-9G JINSON

PRICE CODE 23

Total Square Footage: 2383 Future Expansion 338 Sq. Ft.

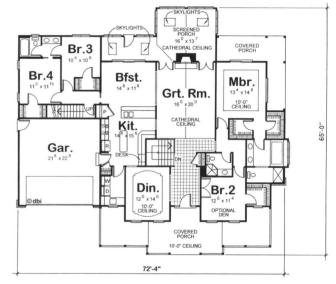

NOTE: 9 FT. MAIN LEVEL WALLS

OPTIONAL DEN

FUTURE EXPANSION

- the dining room's trayed ceiling and windows overlooking the front porch provide a pleasing view from the entry

- a cathedral ceiling and French doors flanking the fireplace give the great room a sense of grandeur

- in the back of the home a spacious screened porch complete with cathedral ceiling and skylights provides the perfect getaway

800-947-7526

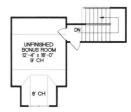

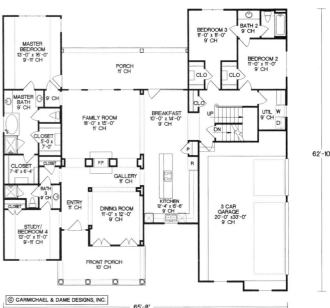

Total Square Footage: 2393 Unfinished Future Room 222 Sq. Ft.

- front porch grants access into entry and dining room which both view a central see-thru fireplace

- the kitchen is loaded with storage and offers an eating bar long enough to seat the whole family

- secondary bedrooms enjoy walk-in closets and share a Hollywood bath

- in the front of the home, a lovely study with angled ceiling converts to a guest suite with secluded access

3514-9G NOTTSBURY
PRICE CODE 23

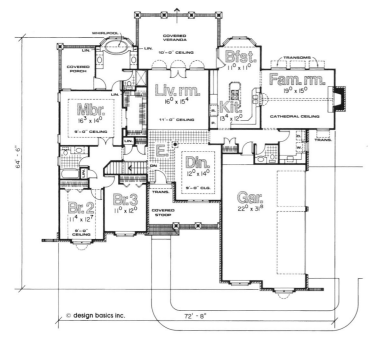

Total Square Footage: 2399

- well designed covered stoop ties together this attractive front elevation

- living room with 11-foot ceiling and French doors leads to covered veranda

- covered porch off master bedroom offers excellent private retreat outdoors

8044-9G FALCON POINT

PRICE CODE 24

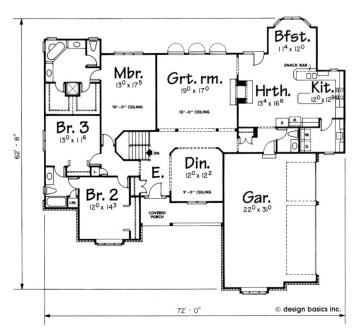

Total Square Footage: 2404

- arched windows, columns, a volume ceiling and a see-thru fireplace enhance the great room

- combined kitchen breakfast area and harth room offer plenty of room for casual entertaining

- the front porch is a great place to while away an afternoon on

- master suite comes with two walk-in closets and spacious bath with corner whirlpool

9159-9G EDGEWATER COURT

PRICE CODE 24

Total Square Footage: 2409

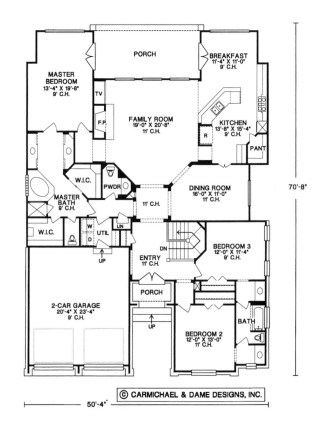

- central corridor produces views from the entry to the rear of the home

- family room enjoys interesting angles, fireplace, built-in entertainment center and ample windows

- back porch is accessed from the breakfast area and master bedroom

- kitchen is highly functional with a peninsula snack bar, walk-in pantry and service counter near the dining room

design basics inc.
HOME PLAN DESIGN SERVICE

Total Square Footage: 2411

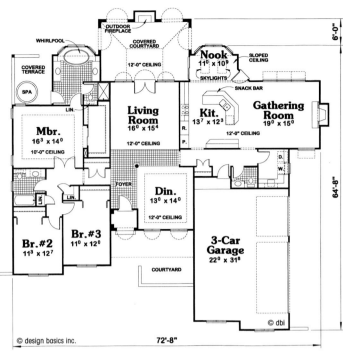

- partially covered courtyard in the front of the home provides a focal point for three tall arched windows in the dining room and foyer

- with arched windows, French doors and a 12-foot ceiling, the open living room has a very spacious feeling

- an outdoor fireplace and a covered courtyard extends the living space in the back of the home

- highlights in the open kitchen, gathering room and nook are transom-topped windows, a fireplace, lengthy snack bar and skylights

© design basics inc.   72'-8"

NOTE: 9 FT. MAIN LEVEL WALLS

1232-9G EVANSTON
PRICE CODE 24

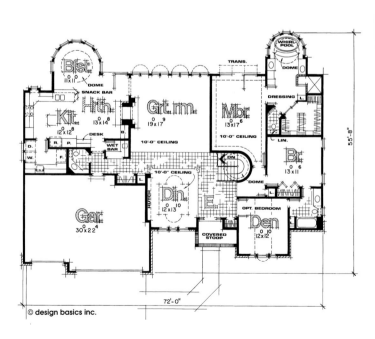

© design basics inc.   72'-0"

CUSTOMIZE
any home plan

Total Square Footage: 2422

- dramatic domed ceilings repeated in stairwell, dinette and master bath

- large master suite includes open shower, special lighting, large walk-in closet and stylish whirlpool

- dining room defined by columns seen from entry

- beautiful great room with repetitive arched windows

24014-9G PEARL
PRICE CODE 24

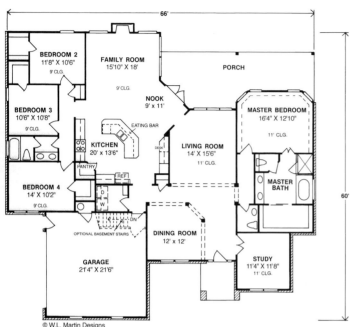

Total Square Footage: 2451

- both the dining room and study in this home offer nearly floor-to-ceiling windows viewing the front

- corner bayed windows provide a rear view in the master bedroom

- the open arrangement of the kitchen, breakfast nook and family room will create a comfortable place to relax

- double doors open to a study neatly tucked in the front of this home

2778-9G COMSTOCK
PRICE CODE 24

Total Square Footage: 2456

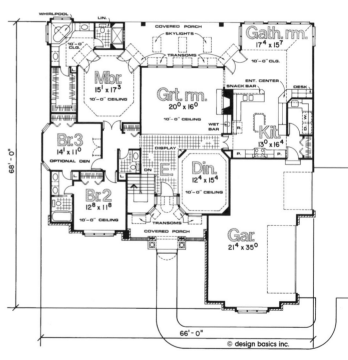

- open great room features wet bar, fireplace and tall windows allowing natural light

- wide kitchen features island, two pantries and easy laundry access

- double doors open to master suite with French doors leading to master bath and covered porch

- master bath with whirlpool, dual-lavs, plant shelves and large walk-in closet

800-947-7526

Total Square Footage: 2467

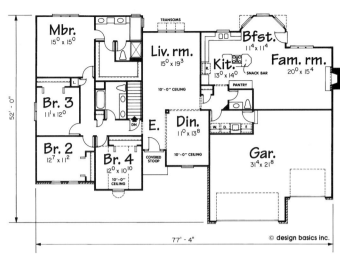

Mbr.
15⁰ x 15⁰

Br. 3
11¹ x 12⁰

Br. 2
12⁷ x 11²

Br. 4
12⁰ x 10¹⁰
10'-0'' CEILING

Liv. rm.
15⁰ x 19³
10'-0''' CEILING

E.

Din.
11⁰ x 13⁸
10'-0'' CEILING

COVERED STOOP

Bfst.
11⁴ x 11⁴

Kit.
13⁰ x 14⁰
SNACK BAR

Fam. rm.
20⁰ x 15⁴

PANTRY

Gar.
31⁴ x 21⁸

52' - 0"

77' - 4"

© design basics inc.

- stone and shake exterior give the feeling of a snug cottage

- all formal rooms are linked for entertaining ease

- bedrooms are separated on a private wing

- kitchen, breakfast area and family room are arranged for seclusion at the back of the home

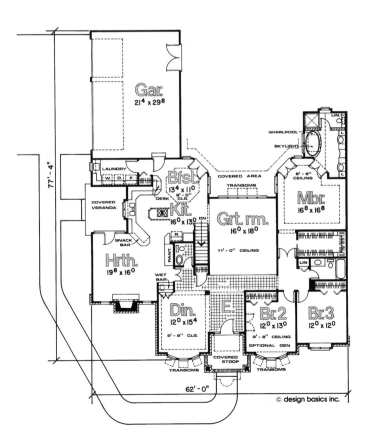

Gar.
21⁴ x 29⁸

77' - 4"

LAUNDRY
W. D. F.

COVERED VERANDA

Bfst.
13⁴ x 11⁰
DESK 9'-0'' CLG.

Kit.
16⁰ x 13⁰

SNACK BAR

Hrth.
19⁸ x 16⁰

WET BAR

WHIRLPOOL
SKYLIGHT

COVERED AREA
TRANSOMS

Mbr.
16⁸ x 16⁸
8'-8'' CEILING

Grt. rm.
16⁰ x 18⁰
11'-0'' CEILING

LIN.

Din.
12⁰ x 15⁴
9'-8'' CLG.

E.

Br. 2
12⁰ x 13⁰
9'-8'' CEILING
OPTIONAL DEN

Br. 3
12⁰ x 12⁰

COVERED STOOP
TRANSOMS   TRANSOMS

62' - 0"

© design basics inc.

Total Square Footage: 2470

- bedroom 2 with optional French doors can be utilized as a den

- gigantic hearth room with snack bar and door to roomy covered veranda

- entertainment-sized kitchen and sunny dinette also ideal for family gathering

- pampering master suite includes doors to outside, boxed ceiling, French doors to dressing area and luxurious bath with whirlpool, dual-lavs and make-up counter

2206-9G HAWKESBURY

PRICE CODE 24

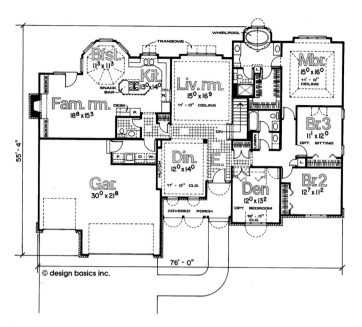

Total Square Footage: 2498

- entry views formal dining room and living room beyond

- gazebo dinette open to family room

- luxurious dressing area in master suite with his-and-her vanities, large walk-in closet and oval whirlpool below windows

- versatile den can become fourth bedroom

- bedroom 3 easily converts to sitting area for master bedroom

- staircase open for future finished basement

3535-9G HALLMARK

PRICE CODE 25

Total Square Footage: 2504

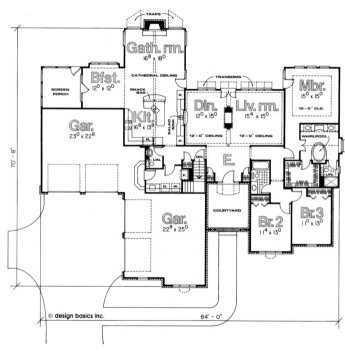

- see-thru fireplace and French doors to back highlight living and dining rooms

- screened in porch located off sunny breakfast area

- kitchen provides snack bar, island counter, easy access to dining room and cathedral ceiling stretching to gathering room

800-947-7526

2652-9G LAWRENCE
PRICE CODE 25

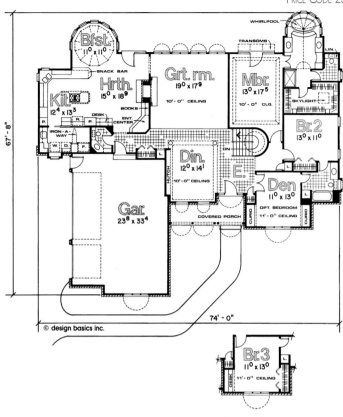

Total Square Footage: 2512

- impressive 12" tapered columns define formal dining room with 10-foot ceiling
- domed ceiling above curved landing for stairs to basement
- French doors open into den with twin curio cabinets or convert den to third bedroom with built-in desk
- curved wall in sumptuous master bedroom with vaulted ceiling

OPTIONAL BEDROOM

9199-9G KINGWOOD SHOWCASE
PRICE CODE 25

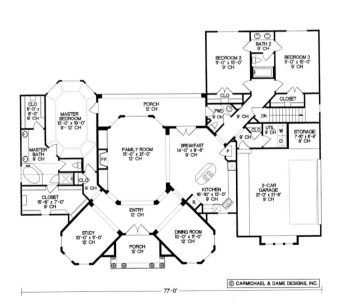

Total Square Footage: 2517

CUSTOMIZE
any home plan

- a dramatic angled floor plan creates long-lasting interest
- master suite is a luxurious retreat with an octagon-shaped bedroom, his-and-her walk-in closets, a dual-lav and a whirlpool tub
- just off the entry, twin rooms comprise the study and dining room
- an interesting family room enjoys a fireplace with built-in cabinets

www.designbasics.com
123

3057-9G ASCOTT

PRICE CODE 25

Total Square Footage: 2538

- grand front porch creates majestic elevation

- living room and bedroom 2/optional den each have 10-foot ceilings

- island kitchen features abundant pantries, lazy Susan and snack bar

- spacious laundry/mud room off kitchen has convenient dual access

- private bedroom wing offers two secondary bedrooms and luxurious master suite featuring spacious walk-in closet with built-in dressers, and private access to back yard

2581-9G EASTRIDGE

PRICE CODE 25

Total Square Footage: 2558

- wide-open formal dining room and great room provide tremendous living space

- atrium door takes you from luxurious master bedroom onto covered deck

- secondary bedrooms complemented by private bath with two vanities

- bayed dinette blends into huge hearth room with fireplace and built-in cabinets

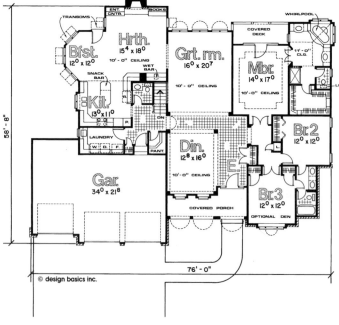

OPTIONAL DEN

design basics inc.
HOME PLAN DESIGN SERVICE

Total Square Footage: 2579

NOTE: 9 FT. MAIN LEVEL WALLS

- the front porch offers a sense of presence through large columns with brick pedestals and double-hung windows with transoms above

- a back porch makes a great place to enjoy an evening outdoors

- sloped ceilings and three double windows bring character to the breakfast area/hearth room

- bedrooms 2 and 3 share a compartmentalized bath with double vanity

5503-9G BRIARTON
PRICE CODE 25

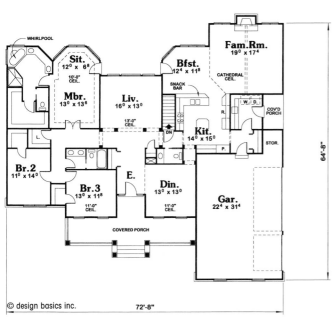

NOTE: 9 FT. MAIN LEVEL WALLS

Total Square Footage: 2586

- columns and dropped soffits frame a view into the living room and the back yard beyond

- an integrated family room and breakfast area will help the family easily circulate with the kitchen

- a walk-in linen closet services the secondary bedrooms and nearby full bath

- extra vanity space in the master bath offers ample space to apply make-up and style

www.designbasics.com

125

3045-9G ROYALE

PRICE CODE 25

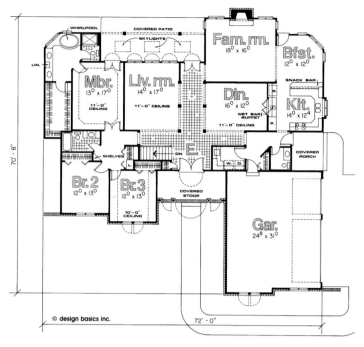

Total Square Footage: 2598

- fantastic kitchen features pass-thru buffet to dining room, two Lazy Susans, and shares snack bar with spacious breakfast area

- side entrance from covered porch located near kitchen and laundry facilities

- dazzling rear elevation created by skylit covered porch with arched windows and French doors to master suite and entry hall

- luxurious trend continues in master suite with oval whirlpool bath, exceptional his-and-her vanities and ample walk-in closet

6806-9G SAN CARLOS

PRICE CODE 26

Total Square Footage: 2647

- convenient features in the kitchen include ample cabinets, a walk-in pantry and a long, angled snack bar

- master suite enjoys boxed ceiling, dual-lav, compartmented bath, corner whirlpool and large walk-in closet

- an open floor plan is ideal for entertaining allowing guests to mingle throughout the great room, kitchen, nook and screened deck

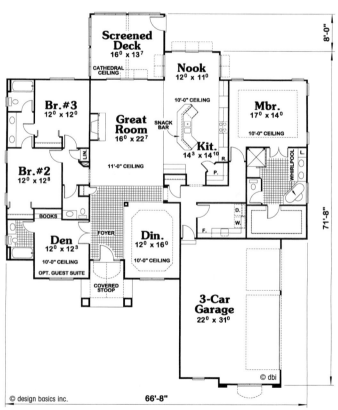

NOTE: 9 FT. MAIN LEVEL WALLS

800-947-7526

Total Square Footage: 2650

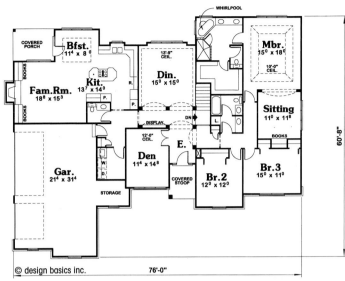

- for those who work at home or catch up on ofice work in the evenings, a den is located just off the entry

- bedrooms 2 and 3 share a handy compartmentalized bath with two vanities

- expanding off the breakfast area is a covered porch

- daily interaction wii be effortless through the open design of the kitchen and family room

NOTE: 9 FT. MAIN LEVEL WALLS

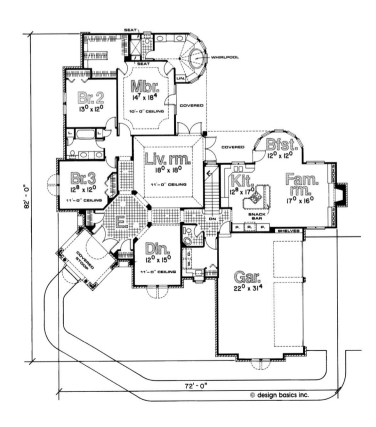

Total Square Footage: 2651

- formal entertaining areas defined by ceiling treatments and flooring materials

- master bath's sunken oval whirlpool under canopy of dramatic sloped

ceiling is surrounded by windows

- living room, master bedroom and dinette/family room offer outside access to covered patios

3483-9G Westmont

PRICE CODE 26

Total Square Footage: 2655

- great room reveals transom windows showcasing a fireplace

- oak breakfast area features bayed windows and 11'-foot ceiling

- kitchen amenities include oak floor, three lazy Susans and abundant counter space

- master suite with vaulted 11'-foot ceiling and access to private covered porch

- bedroom 4 converts easily to a den or mother-in-law suite

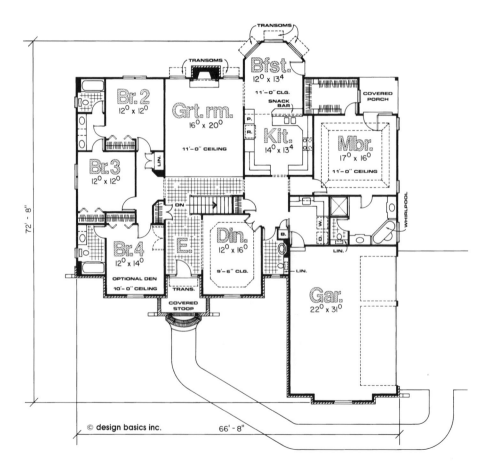

Price Code 26

Total Square Footage: 2679

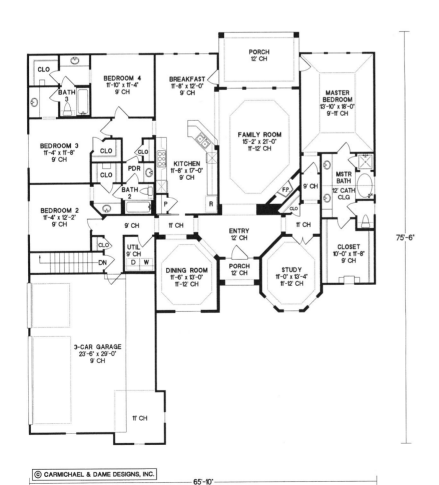

- spacious entry leads to grand family room with tall ceiling, corner fireplace and interesting angles

- convenient features in the kitchen and adjoining breakfast nook include wrapping counters, a pantry, a snack bar and access to the porch

- master suite enjoys access to back porch, vaulted ceiling, his-and-her vanities, whirlpool tub and large walk-in closet with built-in dresser

- all three secondary bedrooms have walk-in closets and private access to a bath

© CARMICHAEL & DAME DESIGNS, INC.

6802-9G VISTA

PRICE CODE 27

Total Square Footage: 2716

- a series of arches are repeated throughout the foyer, great room, dining room and covered courtyard

- arched gates and a lovely fountain add beauty in the courtyard accessed from the dining and gathering rooms

- in addition to a 14-foot ceiling, the great room enjoys a built-in entertainment center

- amenities in the kitchen and adjoining gathering room include lazy Susans, center cooktop with snack bar, two pantries, a built-in desk, and a fireplace

- the master suite enjoys its own, private covered terrace with spa, a kitchenette and his-and-her closets

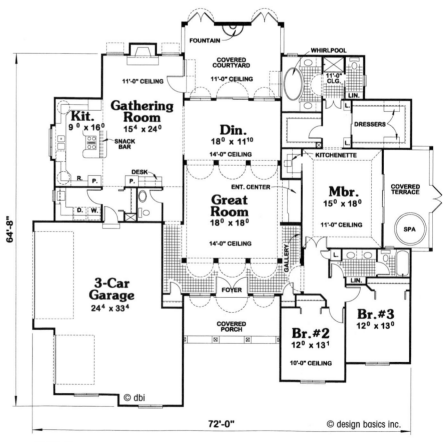

NOTE: 9 FT. MAIN LEVEL WALLS

800-947-7526

design basics inc.
HOME PLAN DESIGN SERVICE

Total Square Footage: 2716

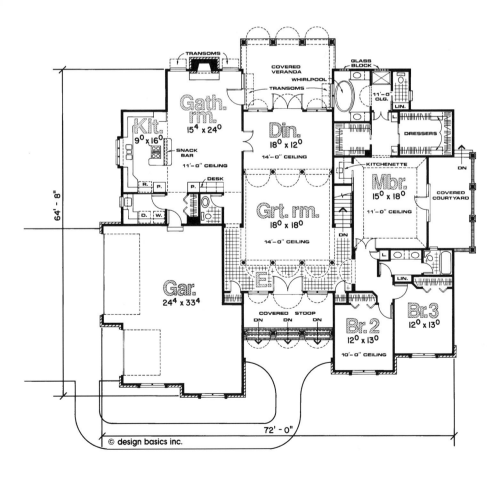

- a series of stunning arches lead from the entry through the volume great room and dining room to the elegant covered veranda

- tall windows flank beautiful fireplace in gathering room with access to covered veranda

- additional outdoor living space provided by private courtyard off master bedroom

- lavish master bedroom includes kitchenette and two walk-in closets

- bedrooms 2 and 3 share spacious compartmented bath with two lavs

CUSTOMIZE
any home plan

5003-9G SAYBROOKE
Price Code 27

Total Square Footage: 2750

- the tapered columns, panel shutters and beautiful arched window treatments of this design offer an influential elevation

- just off the entry, the dining room features double doors that link to the kitchen for serving ease

- the kitchen, with an island and snack bar, serves the breakfast area and great room

- an 11-foot-high ceiling and raised-hearth fireplace distinguish the great room

- bedrooms 2 and 3 are located in the left wing of the home, and share a Hollywood bath

- bedroom 4 — a perfect guest suite — easily converts into a den with double-doors off the entry

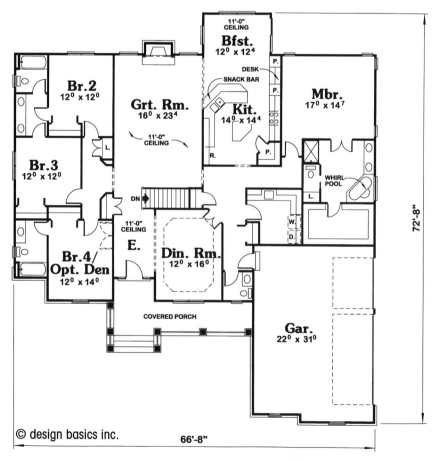

NOTE: 9 FT. MAIN LEVEL WALLS

800-947-7526

Total Square Footage: 2775

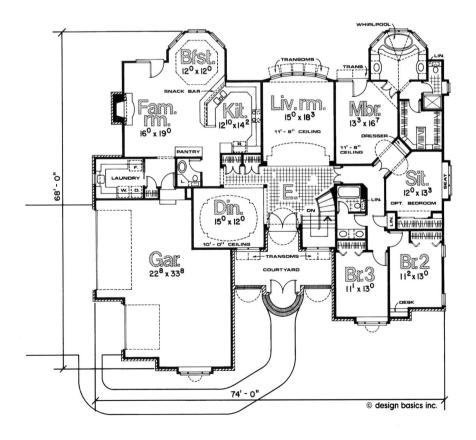

• integrated design of the kitchen, dinette and family room for family living

• for maximum privacy, double doors seclude the bedroom wing from the rest of the house

• luxury abounds in the richly appointed master suite whose character is enhanced by a private sitting room

OPTIONAL BEDROOM

3033-9G AVALON

PRICE CODE 28

Total Square Footage: 2899

- 12-foot-tall entry centers on formal living room with fireplace and beautiful arched windows

- large laundry room with double window, freezer space and laundry sink

- informal living enjoyed in spacious family room and breakfast area

- master suite features his-and-her walk-in closets, a built-in kitchenette and private access to rear yard

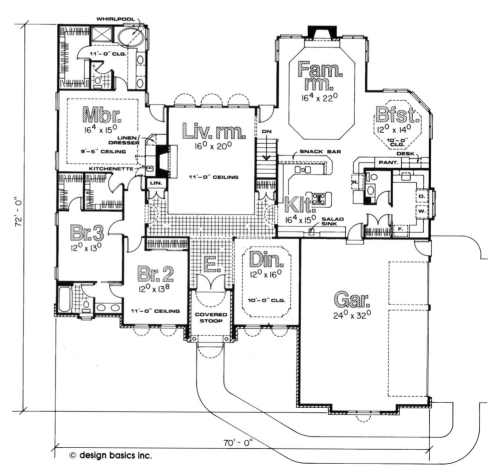

© design basics inc.

800-947-7526

design basics inc.
HOME PLAN DESIGN SERVICE

Total Square Footage: 2988

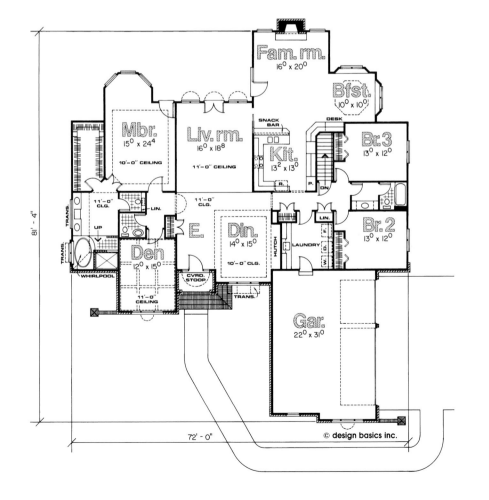

- massive living room with 11'-foot tall ceiling, beautiful arched transoms and French doors with rear access

- secluded den with 11-foot spider beamed ceiling

- kitchen offers a planning desk and angled cabinets with glass doors

- large family room is strategically open to both gazebo breakfast area and kitchen

- master bedroom complemented by bayed sitting area, walk-in closet and access to the back

3018-9G SHILOH
PRICE CODE 29

Total Square Footage: 2994

- gathering room with cathedral ceiling, brick fireplace and entertainment center has useful service porch entrance

- private access to arbor and secluded work space highlight master bedroom

- bedroom 2 can become private study off master bedroom while bedroom 4 easily converts to optional den

OPTIONAL DEN

© design basics inc.

design basics inc.
HOME PLAN DESIGN SERVICE

Total Square Footage: 3312

OPTIONAL
BASEMENT ACCESS

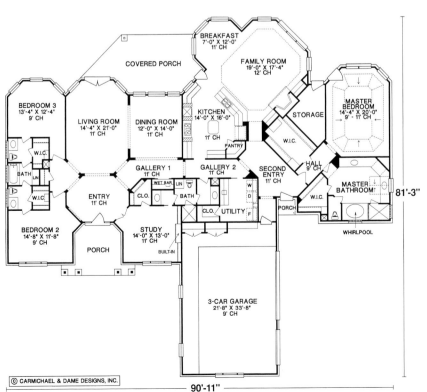

81'-3"

90'-11"

© CARMICHAEL & DAME DESIGNS, INC.

- the living areas of this home enjoy 11 to 12-foot ceilings and interesting angles

- dramatic entry leads to octagon-shaped living room which leads to a covered porch and adjoins the dining room

- amenities in the angled family room include a fireplace flanked with built-in cabinetry, an abundance of windows and a shared snack bar with the kitchen

- luxurious master suite includes his-and-her walk-in closets and vanities and whirlpool tub

- secondary bedrooms enjoy walk-in closets and compartmented bath

9118-9G VILLA DE BACA

PRICE CODE 35

Total Square Footage: 3590

- tall ceilings and an open floor plan in the entry, dining and living rooms and loggia create a tremendous sense of grandeur

- an open kitchen, breakfast area and hearth room allow family and friends to mingle freely; French doors in the breakfast area provide access to the porch

- on the right side of the home a guest suite and bedroom 2 enjoy private baths and walk-in closets

- on the opposite end, master suite includes his-and-her vanities, whirlpool and divided walk-in closet

- with bath nearby, a study in the front of the home could also be used as a bedroom

CUSTOMIZE
any home plan

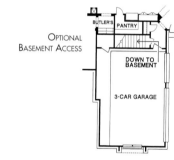

OPTIONAL
BASEMENT ACCESS

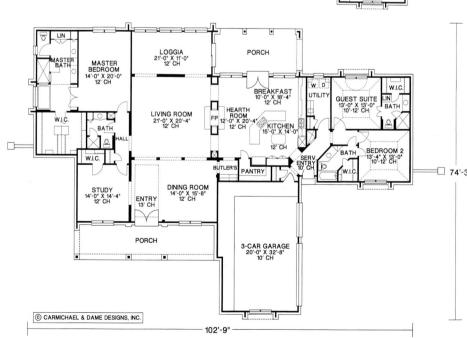

design basics inc.
HOME PLAN DESIGN SERVICE

Total Square Footage: 3734

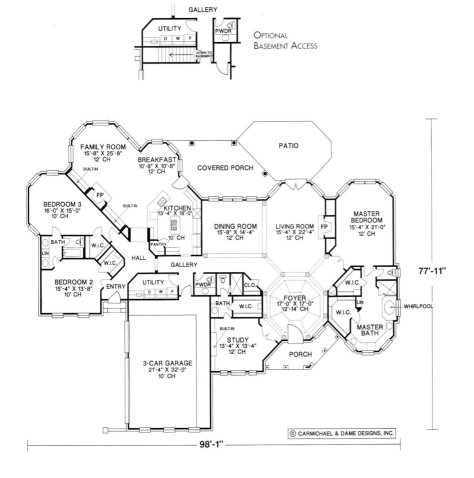

GALLERY

UTILITY
D W F

PWDR

OPTIONAL
BASEMENT ACCESS

DOWN TO BASEMENT

• an octagon-shaped foyer edged with columns sets a grand stage

• columns continue in the open dining room and living room which enjoys a fireplace and access to the patio

• angles and windows adorn the master suite with his-and-her vanities, walk-in closets and a luxurious whirlpool tub

• the family room enjoys an abundance of windows on angled walls and a fireplace flanked with built-in cabinets

• wrapping counters, a center cooktop, a corner pantry and a door to the covered porch highlight the kitchen

FAMILY ROOM
15'-8" X 25'-8"
12' CH

BREAKFAST
10'-8" X 10'-8"
12' CH

PATIO

COVERED PORCH

BUILT-IN

BEDROOM 3
16'-0" X 15'-0"
10' CH

FP

BUILT-IN

KITCHEN
13'-4" X 18'-0"

10' CH

MASTER BEDROOM
15'-4" X 21'-0"
12' CH

FP

DINING ROOM
15'-8" X 14'-4"
12' CH

LIVING ROOM
15'-4" X 22'-4"
12' CH

BATH

W.I.C.

W.I.C.

HALL

PANTRY

GALLERY

W.I.C.

BEDROOM 2
15'-4" X 13'-8"
10' CH

ENTRY

UTILITY
D W F

PWDR

CLO.

FOYER
17'-0" X 17'-0"
12'-14' CH

W.I.C.

LIN

WHIRLPOOL

77'-11"

BATH

W.I.C.

W.I.C.

BUILT-IN

STUDY
13'-4" X 13'-4"
12' CH

MASTER BATH

3-CAR GARAGE
21'-4" X 32'-0"
10' CH

PORCH

© CARMICHAEL & DAME DESIGNS, INC.

98'-1"

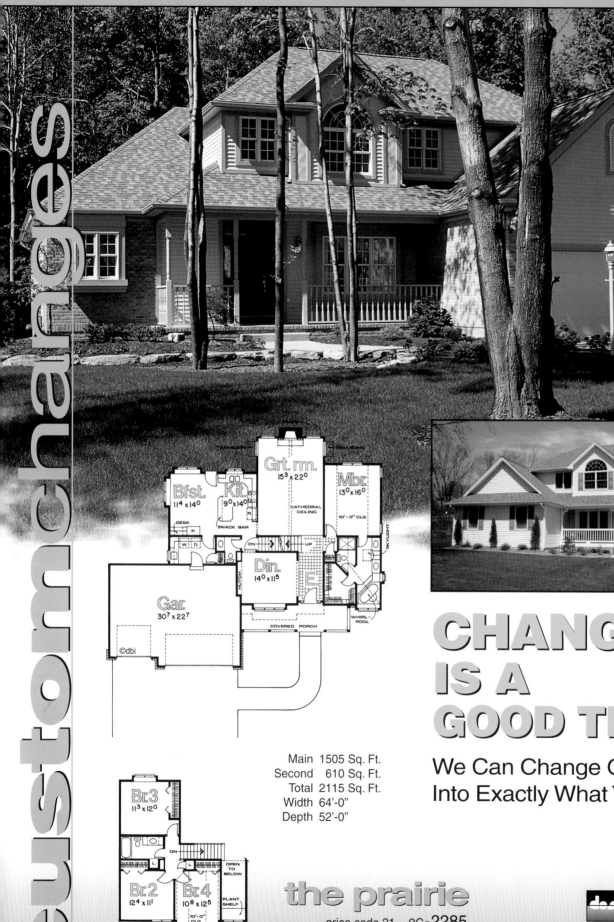

Grt. rm.
15³ x 22⁰
CATHEDRAL CEILING

Bfst.
11⁴ x 14⁰

Kit.
9⁰ x 14⁰

Mbr.
13⁰ x 16⁰
10'- 0" CLG.

DESK

SNACK BAR

P.

W.D.

DN. UP

Din.
14⁰ x 11⁵

HUTCH

SKYLIGHT

WHIRL-POOL

Gar.
30⁷ x 22⁷

©dbi

COVERED PORCH

Main 1505 Sq. Ft.
Second 610 Sq. Ft.
Total 2115 Sq. Ft.
Width 64'-0"
Depth 52'-0"

Br.3
11³ x 12⁰

DN

OPEN TO BELOW

Br. 2
12⁴ x 11¹

Br. 4
10⁸ x 12⁵
10'- 0" CLG.

PLANT SHELF

PLANT SHELF

the prairie
price code 21 9G-2285

CHANGE IS A GOOD THING

We Can Change Our Plans Into Exactly What You Want

custom changes

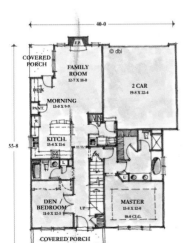

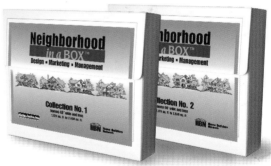

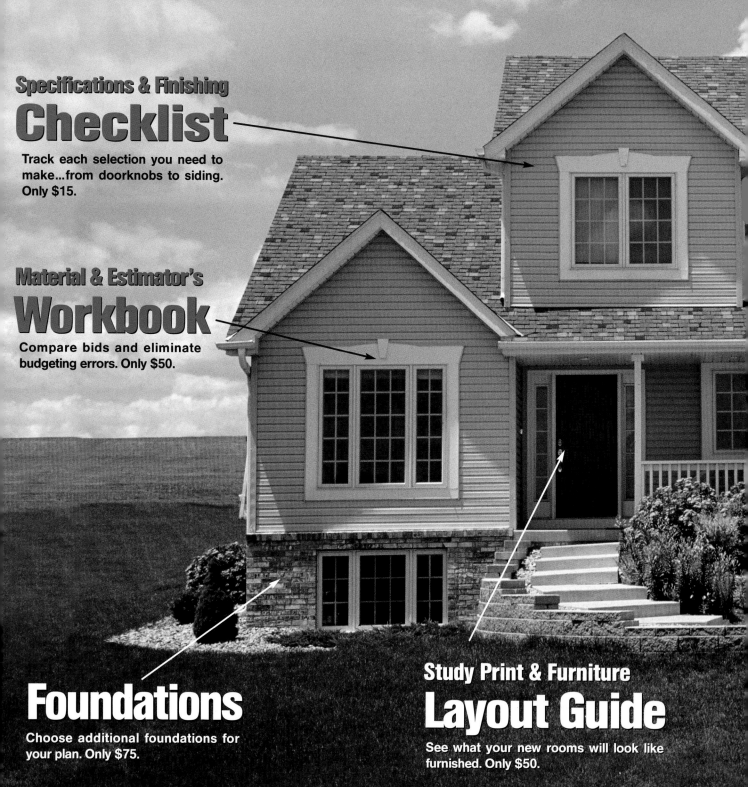

Enhance Your Design Basics Experience
With a Complete Line of Support Materials

Specifications & Finishing
Checklist
Track each selection you need to make...from doorknobs to siding. Only $15.

Material & Estimator's
Workbook
Compare bids and eliminate budgeting errors. Only $50.

Foundations
Choose additional foundations for your plan. Only $75.

Study Print & Furniture
Layout Guide
See what your new rooms will look like furnished. Only $50.

800-947-7526
www.designbasics.com/9G

design basics inc
HOME PLAN DESIGN SERVICE